SO YOU WANT TO BE A MANAGER!

Other Books in This Series

So You Want to Be a Supervisor!
So You Want to Be an Executive!

Other Books by Elton T. Reeves

Management Development for the Line Manager
The Dynamics of Group Behavior

SO YOU WANT TO BE A MANAGER!

Elton T. Reeves

(AMA)

American Management Association, Inc.

© American Management Association, Inc., 1971.
All rights reserved. Printed in the United States of America.

This book may not be reproduced in whole or in part
without the express permission of the Association.

International standard book number: 0-8144-5245-0
Library of Congress catalog card number: 78-138570

Second printing

With love, to my sister,
Amy R. Jencks, who has been waiting
a long time for this

Foreword

THE purpose of this book is to help the first-line supervisor plan and implement a development program which will aid him in becoming a candidate for promotion to middle management. Every attempt has been made to keep the discussions as pragmatic as possible, both in approach and in the examples given.

Elton T. Reeves

Contents

	Introduction	1
1	How Much More Responsibility Do You Want?	18
2	What Is the Job of the Middle Manager?	39
3	How Do You Manage Other Managers?	60
4	What Is the Occupational Disease of the Middle Manager?	80
5	How Are You at Politics?	100
6	What Is the State of Your Development Plan?	121
7	What Evidence Do You Have of Your Promotability?	142
8	How Are Your Peer Relationships?	163
9	How Do You Rate Your Leadership Style?	183
10	What's Your Boss Saying to You?	205
11	Now What Do You Do?	226
	Index	247

Introduction

MOST first-line supervisors, as soon as they have oriented themselves to a supervisory position, feel a resurgence of the personal ambition which made them seek a management job in the first place. They begin to look around and size up the possibility of future promotion. This activity becomes an ongoing part of their business life. The purpose of this book is to delineate the kinds of personal development which will make those future promotions more probable.

What Have You Learned as a First-line Supervisor?

Unless you have learned—and learned well—the functions of management, you are in no position to be thinking of promotion. By now, you should be an expert at planning, both for yourself and for your work group. Although as a first-line supervisor you do most of your planning for relatively short periods of time, it is as necessary for you to do this planning as it is for the company chief executive to map strategy for five years or more downstream. Moreover, you must have some tangible evidence that your planning is consistently pretty good. That is, it must be demonstrably functional.

You have much less latitude in the area of organizing than do managers in higher echelons, but this is another activity that is every bit as necessary for you to do as it is for them. First-line supervisors in companies with elaborate union contracts may be lulled into a false sense of security because they believe that all organizational changes at the hourly level, at least in the manufacturing area, will be governed by provisions of the contract. Nothing could be further from the truth. No matter how restrictive the pertinent clauses may seem to be, the supervisor still enjoys much latitude in making the best possible use of his available manpower.

By this time, you certainly must have learned a great deal about directing your work force. It is in this function that you have succeeded or failed in your day-to-day interpersonal relationships and human skills. You have established the managerial styles in which you can operate most comfortably, and you have developed the one-to-one relationships with your people as individuals which are fundamental to your supervisory operations.

In all probability, you have learned more in the field of controls than in any other management function. Effective controls for any group are a personal matter. Granted that

INTRODUCTION

many of the controls operating within your group have been superimposed by higher management, you still have available a variety of choices to satisfy your personal needs for getting feedback from your operation. As long as those controls are reasonable, and their rationale has been fully explained to your people, they make your operations smoother and more enjoyable.

You have undoubtedly learned more about your company since becoming a supervisor than in all the time you spent before as an employee. There are two reasons for this rapidly acquired knowledge: You have become aware of the things which higher management has decided you must know in order for you to function properly, and your own interest in your work is greater than it used to be. You have discovered that your increased familiarity with the company has made your job much easier. It gives you a much sounder reference point for your daily decision making than your unsupported personal judgments would offer. There is another inherent benefit in your knowledge of the company —your employees turn to you more naturally for company information, thus building a more desirable relationship between superior and subordinate.

It is a safe bet that your functional knowledge of communication has increased tremendously since you became a boss. Had this not been true, you could not have succeeded in your supervisory job. As a line or staff worker you needed to communicate in order to get your job done, but when you became a supervisor your needs in this area were multiplied many times. You discovered that some of your more critical communications involved you with your peers rather than with your subordinates. Much of the more important part of your work is done among your

3

peer group, and since you have no authority over them, your communication with them must be of a high order if you are to get the job done. Moreover, you have found it necessary to do a great deal of coaching and teaching of your subordinates in their communication skills, for both your sake and theirs.

Since your induction into management, you have discovered dozens of new facets and techniques in the job of administration. As you started to get your job organized and began to function effectively, you found many ways of simplifying administrative detail. You had to do this to keep your head above water and to get the job accomplished. The most useful single tool to do this was, you discovered, the magic of delegation. By giving carefully selected administrative chores to some of your better people, you both helped them in their development and freed much time for yourself to perform supervisory activities in the purer sense.

The chances are pretty good that you have done little thinking about this learning process while it was going on. You have been too busy. At this point, the best thing you could do to consolidate your position is to examine carefully and tabulate the kinds and amount of knowledge you have acquired since you became a supervisor. This personal inventory should be taken before you even begin to consider tactics for promotion.

How Is Your Job Going Right Now?

Much more than a learning process has been going on since you became a supervisor. You have been doing a

INTRODUCTION

great deal as well, so much that sometimes you wonder if you have any life at all except that job, which has wound its tentacles about you like an octopus. Of course, you probably have affection for the octopus, all the same.

You have become accustomed to being measured continually against a series of bench marks. Whether you make a product or give a service, the most commonly used measurement of your effectiveness as a supervisor is the productivity of your group. All the way up the managerial hierarchy, you and other supervisors are being compared against production standards which you may or may not have had a hand in determining. In the long run, you and all other supervisors know there can be no real excuse for a failure to produce. Extenuating circumstances don't really exist in the minds of managers; the term is a genial fiction maintained to give an air of reasonableness to a situation basically unreasonable in its demands. Because you know this, you have become accustomed to putting production ahead of every other facet of your performance. Your people know this as well as you do. So, as a smart and competitive supervisor, you know each minute of each working day where your group stands in relation to its production.

You are also aware that your production must be kept within well-defined cost limitations. Only monopolies can afford to be careless about costs, and even they know that they can price themselves out of the market if their costs get too high. As a supervisor, you have learned to install and monitor cost controls within your group until they became second nature to your people. In the area of costs you can display some of the creativity and vision which caused you to be picked as a candidate for supervision in the first place. No one should be as aware as you of your group's performance in costs. You must make continual comparisons with other groups in your own enterprise and with your opposite numbers in other companies. The information is available. Sometimes you may have difficulty getting cost figures of other companies, but a little quiet detective work can almost always dredge up a close estimate of how your competition is doing in costs. You will get the immediate and undivided attention of your superiors when you come to them with suggestions for cutting costs significantly.

The matter of quality of your product is not always as open and shut as your productivity and cost controls. Attitudes toward product quality will be determined by the overall philosophy of your top management. Some enterprises hang their entire reputation and future on acquiring a name for top quality. We all recognize the aura which surrounds the Cartiers and Tiffanys of any field. Other organizations make a calculated decision to balance quality against repeat sales; the technique of planned obsolescence is familiar to everyone. Then there are those companies which have several lines of products, of which one or two may be designed for the carriage trade and the others for mass consumption.

Your job as a supervisor is to know exactly what your management demands in the way of quality, and to do your best to get quality performance from your people to conform exactly to management's wishes. You have no freedom of movement in this area; your personal wishes or those of your employees are not germane. This fact causes considerable unhappiness among large numbers of American workmen; some even rebel absolutely against the necessity of cutting quality to an inferior pattern.

INTRODUCTION

Production, costs, and quality will be the major measures of your performance and that of your people, but they are not the only measures. Another criterion, which is rapidly rising in management's list of priorities, and which only a few years ago would have been dismissed as irrelevant, is your performance in the field of employee relations and public relations. Whether the philosophy of your company tends toward Theory X or Theory Y,* all alert managers now recognize that the nature of their relationships with their people has a direct connection with the profitability of the enterprise. It is good business to have a harmonious working atmosphere in your shop or office. It is bad business to have discord and hostility between labor and management, and even worse to have them in the managerial ranks.

A host of other measurements of managerial ability are grouped in what are called administrative duties. How good are your records? Do you make your management reports on time? Do your people know what they should about policy and procedures? Are your duties in regard to contract administration up to date and in shape?

Whether or not your superiors require you to do so, you should keep a running account of your performance in these areas. You, of all people, must know how your work stacks up if you are interested in advancing further up the ladder. This ongoing inventory of your position against recognized performance measures must be an activity you build into your operation. Of all the people concerned, you are the one who must never be surprised by lack of information about your comparative rating as a supervisor.

* For a discussion of Theory X and Theory Y, see Douglas McGregor, *The Human Side of Enterprise* (New York: McGraw-Hill Book Company), 1960.

A field soldier must know the condition of his equipment before he sets out on a patrol. His life depends on this knowledge; so does your professional life as a supervisor.

Is Your Job Still Stretching You?

No matter how expert a supervisor you may have become, your job should still make you stretch. When any person's employment no longer offers challenge to him, he should think seriously about changing jobs. Naturally enough, most of the challenges are yours to discover and exploit. Like motivation, challenge is not something a boss can provide, since what stretches one man is totally unexciting for another.

Building challenge into your job can become a regular, almost routinized, procedure. Segment by segment, examine your work for areas in which your performance is either a shade below par or barely average. Then study your work habits and your approach to any facet of your job in which you are weak. Set free every creative impulse you have and bend it toward the target of improved performance in that area.

In this case, "you" just might mean your crew rather than yourself. If so, you will be in for a concentrated study of your personnel, starting with their fundamental motivation. What is it about this part of their job which fails to elicit their best efforts? Is it a lack of positive leadership on your part? Or, more simply, could it be traced to substandard or inadequate communication between you and your group? Once you have diagnosed the problem to the best of your ability, the solution will usually become evident. This technique can be applied to any part of the work done in your group, either by yourself or by your people. The most obvious and immediate results of your success in this area will be your own satisfaction. This is one of the higher rewards inherent in any job.

Another excellent source of job stretch is in the naturally competitive situation arising among members of a peer group. Tacitly or overtly, your fellow supervisors will often throw down a gauntlet for you to pick up. If your instincts as a fighter are average or better, you will accept the challenge. Moreover, your people will become easily involved in the action if you communicate what the other group is saying and implying. No more ideal situation exists for getting commitment and involvement of your crew than an informal contest with another department in production, sales, quality, safety, or what have you. The only caution to be observed here is one familiar to any experienced supervisor: Too avid a pursuit of this engagement with the "enemy" will produce tunnel vision, and a concomitant danger of straying from the pursuit of major organizational objectives. In addition, too serious a competition can result in enduring enmities. It is your job as the leader to keep a check on natural enthusiasm so that it does not get out of hand.

We said that your superior will not personally be able to put challenge into job for you, any more than he can personally motivate you. However, in your normal contacts with him, many occasions will occur which can trigger a stretch in your job. In day-to-day communication, you may suddenly become aware of an area where you can make a little extra contribution to achieving the overall goals of your boss. Picking up this sort of cue and developing it properly can only improve your superior's opinion of your performance. Handling this opportunity may take extra finesse on your part, since the contribution you make may well be in someone else's work area. If this is the case, you can make yourself doubly a hero if you arrange matters so that your boss knows who is responsible, but also so that the other supervisor involved gets public credit for the achievement. This kind of serendipity may be your good fortune; and you may be the cause of its happening elsewhere.

Job excitement is generated by the state of mind of the jobholder more than by anything else. This is another way of saying that it is mandatory to maintain a youthful outlook on life. It is the young who become excited often and naturally. One aspect of the supervisor's job is especially conducive to maintaining a youthful frame of mind: his frequent posture as a teacher. Good teachers are young in mind, whatever their chronological age and that of their pupils. The young are resilient; the youthful mind is, too. The best weapon anyone can develop against the frustrations of the bewildering changes we face is to preserve a young mental approach to life.

One of the better ways to strengthen the challenge of your job is to compare notes frequently with fellow supervisors, and to make value judgments about the methods they use in this critical aspect of your work life. With very slight or even no modifications, you can often apply a colleague's method to your own operation with considerable gratification. Furthermore, if you in turn communicate one of your successes to a peer, and he becomes excited about it, your own appreciation for the technique will be heightened.

INTRODUCTION

Essentially then, unless job challenge is maintained at all times, life becomes unbearably stale and flat. Yet, no one can provide this impetus for you. You must be the author of the zest you get from your work, and your enthusiasm must be an integral part of your personality on the job.

What Are You Doing to Enrich Your Job?

In a sense, the discussion above dealt with job enrichment, but there is more to the subject than the stretch which should be a part of every job. Frederick Herzberg's concept of job enrichment* assumes "vertical loading," which is an increase in the amount of the action of the job. To enrich your job, you must grow and develop in your own personality during the process. You will gain greater perspective and satisfaction from an enriched job.

Of course, none of this is possible without your superior's full and ongoing cooperation, because the changes will be so great as to make your job almost unrecognizable. You must be given greater authority, and you must increase delegation noticeably to make enrichment happen. By the same token, your people will be involved, because your job cannot change to such an extent without touching them quite deeply. To enrich your job as a supervisor, start with an industrial engineering study of several jobs of your people, in order to determine where the greatest possibility for improvement lies.

* The reader interested in pursuing this concept would do well to read Frederick Herzberg's article in the Jan.–Feb. 1968 issue of the *Harvard Business Review*, entitled: "One More Time—How Do You Motivate Your Workers?"

If your organizational structure and operations have been more or less average, the process of job enlargement within your area will actually be traumatic for you, even though you know what is going on and approve heartily. As your people assume more responsibility, and carry through on their work assignments with more autonomy, it will seem to you at first that your job is being cut from under you. And that is true—that is, your *old* job. You will have to readjust your activities to do more of the things a supervisor should do, rather than occupying your time with petty chores not worthy of your status and pay. Once this change has been made, you will perceive vistas and possibilities to your job which you have never known before.

Although the underlying reason for taking on this project may appear to be selfish, job enrichment in your area will help those who work for you and all the organization above you. The first step is an educational one. The project will never succeed unless everyone concerned knows exactly what is planned, and what benefits are being sought. Enlightened management will not usually be hard to sell, since the payoff will be in dollars of profit as well as personal satisfactions. However, your people may present some problems, since they will see at once that they will probably be working harder at the end than they have been accustomed to. But if they are mature human beings, they will, without fail, embrace the prospect of more autonomy and more status in their work, and will prove their ability to follow through, from inception to completion, on an increment of the total job. The project can provide answers to their many unspoken questions about their

INTRODUCTION

personal worth and the value of their jobs to the organization.

Such a fascinating activity carries with it a danger of engendering much impatience in all concerned. You must remember that results will, in all probability, be quite slow in coming. In fact, as Professor Herzberg points out, at first there will inevitably be a drop in production and overall efficiency, while the changed jobs are being restructured in the minds of the workers. Panic must not be allowed to take over, since this period is usually rather short, and then the improvement will come with startling swiftness.

There are two reasons why you, the supervisor involved, should initiate this action. The main reason is that you will then be in an unassailable position for claiming the credit for the resultant improvements, and this can do nothing but enhance your general reputation. The second reason is purely psychological: You will be more deeply involved and committed to an idea which you conceived and initiated, and your chances for success will be much greater because of the greater efforts you will invest.

There is another result of this job enrichment activity which should not be forgotten. In most cases, you will find it necessary to redesign completely the controls for your work group. Changes in procedures and in job relationships will be so great that the old controls will simply no longer be functional. You should not hesitate to seek professional advice about controls. Experts in methods and systems do this sort of work for a living; they are totally involved, and they bring to control design both training and experience. Make use of their services with discretion, and you will have a better operation more quickly after your job enrichment program has been installed.

The net result of a successful foray into this arena will be that you have effectively made yourself a member of middle management without even being promoted, since your people will now be doing many of the things a first-line supervisor has traditionally done. In other words, you will have an opportunity to explore the work area toward which your ambitions are pointing without assuming the extra risks an actual promotion involves. It is somewhat like the situation you were in if you came up via the temporary foreman route. This experience can be a really exciting and productive part of your supervisory work life.

Shall We Take a Look Upstairs?

If you have made a complete evaluation of your present job status along the lines indicated, perhaps it is now time to take a look up the sides of Mount Olympus. It is always a little frustrating to try to evaluate another person's job, but you must try to do so before you can make a valid judgment as to whether you still want to be considered as a candidate for advancement. Whatever your decision, you will have done yourself a signal service by clarifying the situation. If you opt for further advancement, you will have a clearly defined development program to lay out; if you decide that you have reached your safe haven, there are other things you can do to maintain the security of your present position. In either event, your peace of mind is at stake, and you must clarify your own thinking in order to continue to function well on your present assignment.

INTRODUCTION

You will always feel a little uncomfortable while making value judgments about the middle manager's job. Perhaps the best approach is to go to some of your friends who are middle managers and lay your cards on the table. If you have their goodwill, you can count on their help.

Obviously, your first target will be to delimit the main differences between their job and yours. Are they differences of degree or of basic nature? How have your friends found their personal operations differing since entering the middle manager's job? Your sampling of resource personnel should be fairly wide—never be satisfied with only one or two reports. It will be your chore to synthesize several responses into a picture of what you may expect if you become a member of middle management.

Just as important to your final decision will be the determination of the similarities between your job and theirs. What do they still do routinely that you also do? One area which should be probed deeply and effectively is that of delegation. Remember, as a manager of managers, you will have supervisors reporting to you, and their ability to take on new responsibilities will be measurably greater than will that of your subordinates. That is, it will be greater if your subordinates are doing their jobs. Once more, the matter of controls becomes important. If you delegate, you must always remember that you cannot delegate away responsibility; you are going to have to inspect at regular intervals the performance of your people in their areas of delegation. You will not have gained too much in personal time, but you will have magnified your effectiveness many times by having practiced proper delegation.

At the risk of being repetitive, we should reinforce the

necessity of checking all steps of this process with your immediate superior. At this point, it would be fatal to your hopes to give the slightest indication that you are bypassing or undercutting him. He is your guide and mentor in at least the same depth as your supervisor was when you were an hourly worker or an individual contributor; his interest in your future will be genuine and deep. Incidentally, this positive indication of a continuing and active ambition can do you no harm in his eyes, since his performance is still judged in a major sense by the progress of his men. You will be making him look good by pushing—through channels—for promotion.

Remember that this survey is purely preliminary. You will still have to lay out for yourself a realistic and attainable development program before you start to worry your superiors about promotion.

As you should have suspected by now, all this effort will entail a significant amount of your personal time. Not too much of the procedure can be accomplished on the job; you are much too busy to allow for much divergence from your daily routine. Ambition is a hard taskmaster, and will demand your best efforts as long as you recognize ambition as a major factor in your life. Actually, the building of this process into your total efforts will be another of the many tests to which you will be subjected before you are again promoted.

How Do You Plan for Promotion?

Ten salient features must be acknowledged and prepared for in your attack on the objective of membership in middle management. This book will explore those features and establish ground rules for your attack on the citadel. The one unavoidable aspect of the whole situation is the planning necessary before you start. If ever this management function has had real meaning for you, it is at this stage of your career. The only logical and defensible method is for you to lay out a master plan for getting yourself ready for promotion in the least possible time, with the least possible wasted effort, and with no thought of luck as a decisive factor in your future. It would be fatuous to deny that some promotions are not fortuitous; it would also be foolish to depend on this wild chance for the balance of your personal future. Luck happens to those who are ready for its favors.

Perspective becomes of overweening importance at this juncture. You must maintain a priority of parts in the mosaic of your existence; you have no excuse for allowing tunnel vision to distort your judgment, and you should constantly reevaluate your situation to assure yourself of this objectivity. One of the more easily forgotten aspects of the panorama is the development of your subordinates. This is a good time to remind yourself that you'll never go up until you can replace your own position.

How Much More Responsibility Do You Want?

ONE of the more cogent determinants of whether you want to or should be promoted is the amount of tension under which you customarily operate in your present position. It is quite possible for a supervisor to work day after day under extreme tension and not even be aware of it. What comes to be a way of life seems normal, no matter how far from the median it may be.

What Is Your Present Consumption of Antacids?

There are many differing individual responses to the stimulus of personal tension. A recognizable number of people never get into high gear unless extreme pressures are applied. The process of production of adrenaline by the human body and its release into the bloodstream results in some unpleasant physiological reactions. An increased pulse rate, a feeling of flushing or warmth, and an increased rate of respiration are body conditions which we associate with either fear or anger. The body secretes adrenaline under the stress of those two emotions.

If, by conscious control, you learn to ignore these particular symptoms, the body may show its response to stress in other ways. Finger tapping, quickly moving eyes, rapid or slightly disoriented speech, nervous tics, pacing about the room—the list of the ways in which human beings express stresses can be extended almost indefinitely. As we said, the person himself may not be consciously aware that he is under pressure. Of course, the two extreme bodily reactions to continued stress we all fear are strokes and heart attacks. You would do well to assess your own behavior so that you will become aware of the presence of extra pressures whenever they occur in your work environment. This awareness is pure self-protection, and is of increasing importance to you as you advance in years.

How Much Pressure Can You Take?

Naturally, your mental attitude toward your job is one key to your judgment of this matter. Do you really like your job, or are there several days a month when the prospect of going in to work is almost more than you can face? Are there any individual parts of your job which upset you? Are you frequently angered by the actions of either your superiors, your subordinates, or your peers? Do you still think of your job as glamorous and even exciting? Do you think your subordinates and your fellow supervisors like you? Do you like and respect them, or do you think they are a bunch of clucks?

Candid and honest answers to these questions will reveal much about your response to pressures. We should face the facts: A supervisor is under pressure almost continuously, and will be as long as he remains in his position. Pressure is inherent in his work. The principal and ongoing element of pressure is, of course, the relentless ticking of the clock. There is no way of avoiding or sidestepping a time deadline, and time is the unquestioned master of the business and industrial world. All members of management are slaves to it, and there will never be any release from this condition of servitude. Moreover, the cold facts of the situation are that the pressure will increase noticeably with every step up the hierarchy.

The decision of how much of this pressure you can tolerate is a purely personal one. *But you must make the decision before you decide to continue to press for promotion.* No advantage of going up the ladder can compensate for your inability to continue to operate under heavier stress. You could logically argue that you will never know your tolerance for pressure until you get a chance to test it, and that is technically correct. However, many supervisors make a considered value judgment that for this or a number of other good reasons, they have gone far enough, and will be content to remain where they are.

We would be remiss, however, to leave the impression that a man cannot train himself to adjust to stress. He can.

In the main, stress is caused by a fear of the unknown. When we can see the face of the enemy, we usually start to operate efficiently; when we cannot see him, fear takes over. Thus, the first step in your mental reconditioning is to be sure you recognize the possible booby traps along your road. Once they have been identified, you can take steps to circumvent them, or to avoid them completely. Next in urgency is to make as calm and dispassionate an appraisal as you can of their threat to you. It is often possible even to calculate the probability of the occurrence of an undesirable event, and you will be pleasantly surprised to learn how frequently this probability is extremely low.

By all odds the greatest ally you have in avoiding situations of stress is to do a decent job of planning for all the negative contingencies you can dream up. If you have a tenable plan of action for any threat you could ever face, your mental state will be as light as a feather, even in the face of the knowledge that your plans could be less than perfect. You can't win them all, but you can add a hundred points to your batting average by taking your planning activities seriously.

The logical next step is to get your people into the act with you. They also need to know what they are facing, for they share every risk you face, and their futures are indissolubly entwined with yours. You have a team—use them. The beautiful thing about it is that many times the careful consideration of their inputs may give you just the solution you needed for one of your bigger problems.

An assessment of your ability to function well under fire, plus a knowledge of how much more exposure to artillery there is at the next level, will make it possible for you to determine whether the game is worth the candle.

So You Want to Be a Manager!

How Much Homework Are You Doing Now?

Chances are better than even that ever since you became a supervisor you have been taking work home with you at irregular intervals. Things pile up so high at the office that you just can't seem to get everything done on time. The matter of living your job during your every waking minute can be looked at two ways. If you truly love your work, and are completely contented to be a member of management, doing a little extra at night or on the weekends may not bother you. You may even find satisfaction in knowing that you have planned a little better, or have written a more polished report, or have completed your records a few days ahead of the deadline. The other possibility is that the necessity, real or fancied, of taking work home will add to the pressures on you until they pass the point of tolerance. If the latter is your situation, you should take a serious, long look at the desirability of any further promotions.

If you take work home one night a week now, you would find the frequency tripled or quadrupled if you were to become a middle manager. These solid citizens really carry most of the load of running the enterprise. They implement the policy dreamed up on mahogany row; they are the direct contact with you, who are on the firing line; their duties in communication are of the utmost importance to smooth operations throughout the hierarchy. No matter how well the middle manager is able to delegate, or how efficient his staff personnel are, there are literally thousands of details over a year's time which can never be properly handled except by the boss himself. The days are not long enough to get them all attended to

HOW MUCH MORE RESPONSIBILITY DO YOU WANT?

during office hours, so his attaché case gets a little scuffed and worn looking from constant use.

There are those rare individuals who seem to perform miracles on the job, and who leave the office each day with empty hands and a light heart. Never mind about them. They are in the same category as those best-hated people you used to know in school who got straight A's without doing homework. In one sense of the word, they are not your competition at all. If they put their minds to it, and are really dedicated to their work, they will outstrip all their peers and will be jet propelled upward. The other management personnel will compete with each other in the ways with which most of us are familiar.

At the risk of sounding alarmist, we should note that every indicator points toward one inevitable conclusion: As technology continues to grow more complex, the attendant detail work will also proliferate. Thus, all managers can expect to take more work home in order to stay even with its flow past their desks. Although serious efforts will be made to shorten the span of control, thereby simplifying the manager's job a little, this maneuver simply won't do the whole job of relieving the manager of his paperwork.

Every person has a slightly different tolerance to this situation. It is the additional duties of after-hours work which eventually cause a man or woman to be overworked. Many people never know—or they lose sight of—the fact that a sedentary desk job uses calories and drains physical energy just as much as does manual labor. The office worker needs only slightly fewer calories per day than does the manual laborer. And, because the office worker does not indulge in heavy physical activity, he may easily get into bad eating habits and fail to get proper nourishment.

Even more debilitating—and harder on the body—are the mental and emotional drains associated with continued after-hours work. Human minds and spirits are like storage batteries: They need regular periods of inactivity in order to maintain a proper charge.

The pertinent questions at this point are: How much overtime are you currently putting in on the job, and how much more could you handle on a continuing basis without danger of breakdown? You will be required to make some value judgments in answering these questions, because they can affect your ambitions and the future of your career. Consultation with your family physician is mandatory before you make a final decision about going on up the ladder. Mass communications have done a good job of convincing most people of the necessity of preventive medicine and long-range planning for the maintenance of health. The worst violators of these truths have for years been members of management.

Your boss, if he is wise, will also be keeping a weather eye on this facet of your job. Because of his own situation, he knows better than you do at this point the effects of taking work home continuously. His interest in you, whether personal or purely business, would indicate that he counsel you if he feels you are overdoing things. And you would do well to listen to him.

If you have a problem in this area, or anticipate one in the near future, the answer is, of course, closer attention to your performance of all the management functions, plus some creative work on streamlining and making more efficient your job complex. Your present responsibilities will

HOW MUCH MORE RESPONSIBILITY DO YOU WANT?

never lessen as long as you are in this job; they will increase heavily if you are again promoted. This is one of the key areas affecting your decision about the future. Treat it with the respect it deserves, so that you will have a reasonable chance of doing the right thing if you are offered a step up the ladder.

Do You Feel Comfortable Among Your Peers?

One of the more disconcerting discoveries you made shortly after your promotion to supervision was that some of your peers had anything but a friendly attitude toward you. It helped a little to learn later that there was nothing personal in this—you represented new, fresh competition, and they already had about all of that they wanted. Because of this attitude on the part of some, you took longer than you had anticipated to settle into your new environment. In fact, no matter how long you have been in supervision, the odds are high that you still have reason to doubt the goodwill of several of your peers. They just aren't with you.

There are explanations for this, of course. As we said, you represent part of their competition, and if they are quite ambitious, that is reason enough. Deeper than that, however, is the fact that unfriendly behavior often indicates a basic insecurity on their part. They are less than sure of themselves in their job operations, in their interpersonal relationships, and even in the tenancy of their present jobs, let alone in the possibility of future promotion.

Both general and specific assessments of your peer relationships are essential to your own development plans. One thing is going for you: It would have been nearly impossible for you to have passed the first inspections of your work as a supervisor if a majority of your peers had been united against you. Your management is concerned about smoothness of operations, and a squabbling group of supervisors is not conducive to good results. The fact that you did survive essentially means that at least a bare majority of other supervisors have accepted you into their ranks. Working under this assumption, your program then becomes one of trying to increase your number of friends among them without sacrificing your working standards and without failing to meet your objectives. Putting goodwill from your fellows ahead of this fundamental necessity would be fatal, and all concerned are aware of this fact.

For every echelon you rise in the hierarchy, you will find the competition increasing geometrically. As the platforms up the side of the pyramid grow shorter, the efforts required to keep your footing on them will spiral. However, there are some things you can do to ease your own personal pressures. One of them is to go a little further than you might think necessary to show a spirit of cooperation with other supervisors. They depend on you to help them get their job done, just as you look to others for the same kind of a hand. If you have to spend an unconscionable amount of your energy eliciting this help, your total job becomes much harder. This is as true for them as it is for you; good sense dictates that all supervisors give a hand whenever they reasonably can for the good of all concerned, to say nothing of the enterprise in general.

A second method which can pay good dividends in peer

relationships is to study your peers as individuals, just as you do your own employees. The more you know about each of them as a person, the more predictable their behavior will become to you. If you know how a man thinks and acts, you can learn to avoid situations which will trigger his hostility. On the positive side, if you know his likes, you can easily chart a line of approach. He will respond as positively as you do when someone approaches you by way of your favorite thinking. If you are open and candid in trying to learn these things about your peers, your results will usually be better. They will have no quarrel with you if they think you are pursuing acquaintance with them so that both of you can be helped. It is when hidden agendas are discovered that enmities are born and nurtured.

There could be inherent good in making a formal study of social and industrial psychology at this stage of your career. Experts in this area of the behavioral sciences have been extremely active for the past twenty years, and are close to some fundamental truths about the manner in which people interact in groups. The more you know about this, the easier it will be for you to establish and maintain a viable working relationship with a large percentage of your peers.

Your subordinates can be a big help to you in getting perspective on your peers. If you have an open, two-way relationship with your people, and keep your eyes and ears open when you are with them, you will learn a lot about other working areas and the supervisor responsible for them. The people on the line talk a lot with each other; reputations of bosses are in the public domain for the taking, if you are alert. Of course, this works both ways; the way your people think of you will be as available to your peers as the way their people think of them. The important thing for you is to maintain an easy, unstrained alert while with your people, and then to make use of the information readily at hand.

This matter of peer relationships weighs heavily in the building of the entire working climate. We sometimes get to thinking of each work unit as a separate, cell-like entity sufficient unto itself. This can no more be effective than for an individual to live for and by himself in today's complex society. We have become so interdependent that we cannot survive without the acquiescence of many other people. About the only areas left for the rugged individualist are those of the intellect and the spirit. These can remain inviolate forever, but for day-to-day living, we are forced to get and give cooperation, and to keep a generally supportive attitude in our approach to others. Basically, we have come full circle back to one of man's oldest precepts: the Golden Rule.

What Is Your Level of Action Initiation?

Management personnel vary widely in the level at which they initiate action. Incredible though it may seem, some supervisors wait to be told before they ever make a move on any problem. This, of course, is abdication at the lowest level. Only in the most rigidly centralized type of operation could such lack of action by a supervisor be condoned, and even then, there is no real reason for his job

HOW MUCH MORE RESPONSIBILITY DO YOU WANT?

to exist. If his superior has to come to him with a direct order for action, he might just as well go on down the line to where the work is done, and tell the people directly. Naturally, this type of (mis)management is rarely observed.

Just one step above it is the situation where the supervisor goes to his boss with a problem, and asks for a solution. At least he recognizes that something is wrong, but is afraid to commit himself by suggesting action. In a manner of speaking, he stands before his boss with his hat in his hand, saying "Beggin' your pardon, sir, but what do I do now?" This posture is only slightly less pitiable than the first one mentioned. Of course, from the standpoint of personal security, this supervisor is quite safe. He has the superior's stamp of approval beforehand on whatever is done, and he can never be blamed for the results if they are less than salutary.

About in the middle of the spectrum is the supervisor who suggests a course of action, and awaits approval before making a move. At least he doesn't come with a problem; he presents a plausible solution for what he has recognized as a bottleneck to the organization. He can also be given credit if his suggested course of action turns out to be right.

Next to the top of the heap is the man who sees the problem, picks the best solution, takes the necessary action, and then apprises his superior of what has taken place. This technique requires a rather special relationship between the two of them, namely, mutual trust and confidence. Unless the boss recognizes good judgment and competent leadership in his subordinate, this kind of management can never work. Also, the subordinate must be sure of this feeling from his boss before he is willing to risk his career. To many people, this represents the ideal relationship between levels in the hierarchy, and the best possible kind of management.

Be that as it may, there is still one more possibility—that of the supervisor who sees the problem, defines his best course of action, takes it, and doesn't even bother to report it to his superior. This is just as incredible as the first situation described. Actually, it represents the ultimate in decentralized operation, where the manager is given total and final authority for his area, but remains totally and finally accountable for overall results. There are obviously some bugs in this setup. Communications become so sparse and incomplete that the superior doesn't really know what is going on. He is subject to repeated embarrassment by being questioned about operations in his own area about which he is totally uninformed, and nothing can be more maddening.

It might help to put the question of your level of action initiation into perspective by relating these possible situations to the grid. The latter one, where the supervisor feels he has total autonomy, could only happen under 9.9 leadership style.* No other kind of superior would ever tolerate this kind of action. If you act and then report, you are somewhere in the quadrant between the 5.5 and the 9.9, say, 7.7. As we said, for the good of the whole this can be a productive and viable relationship between you and your boss. The middle way, wherein you go to your boss with a suggested solution, is pure 5.5. This supervisor plays a

* For a complete explanation of the managerial grid, see Robert R. Blake and Jane S. Mouton, *The Managerial Grid* (Houston: Gulf Publishing Co.), 1964.

HOW MUCH MORE RESPONSIBILITY DO YOU WANT?

delicate balancing act among the pressures from above, below, and the sides. The man who throws the question to the boss and lies in wait for an answer is 9.1, and nothing else. He will protect himself to the last ditch, and never find himself out on a limb with a saw in his hand. Finally, as you have already anticipated, the man who waits to be told is 1.1 (great gray abdicator). He, too, will protect himself to the last ditch, except that by his passive inactivity he will suggest repeatedly his own uselessness to his superiors.

There are, nevertheless, some tricky choices to be made among these possibilities for you as a supervisor. They will be governed in the final analysis by the current philosophy of management in your enterprise. You must have the proper sensitivity to know what this philosophy is, and then to respond accordingly. This does not mean that you have no freedom of choice. It is entirely possible that your superiors will tolerate some deviation from accepted procedure if they see in you promise of great potential. All progress is the result of deviation, and your management may be smart enough to recognize this fact. At some point—or at several—in your career, you will have to take a deep breath and decide whether you are going to go along with the mob, or whether you will make the break and opt for a significant change in procedures. These times are ulcer breeders, but they are also career determinants, and your sensitivity as to when you should deviate will in a large measure tell how far up the ladder of management you will eventually go. The one thing to remember is that you must be right in the decisions you make at these times. There is no room for tolerance of error under such circumstances. Either you are right, or you are dead.

So You Want to Be a Manager!

Do You Ever Avoid Your Boss?

Speaking of responsibility, could it be that you already have too much for your stomach? When was the last time you found yourself avoiding your boss because of an unfinished commitment or an unmet deadline? The most common and predictable behavior in such situations would be to take evasive action.

The imposition of controls by your superior is unpleasant to you only when you are aware of deficiencies in your performance. If you are on top of the game, and have a completely clear conscience, you will welcome his checking —even take pride in displaying your accomplishments for his approbation. Of course, you could have other reasons for avoiding your boss, but there is usually some connection between this behavior and your overall record of accomplishment.

Actually, retreat from unfulfilled obligation is the poorest response you could make. The heaviness of the hand of your superior will be in direct proportion to your unavailability at the time he was looking for an accounting. It's the same old story: When you are irritably looking for an errant child, your punishment of him will be milder if you find him immediately than if he hides and takes more of your time in running him down. Better to face the music than a firing squad.

A second observation about this evasive tactic is that it is a clear and visible admission of guilt. You are copping a plea before you have been formally accused of a crime. The jury will find it unnecessary to leave the room, and the judge will not declare a recess before passing sentence.

HOW MUCH MORE RESPONSIBILITY DO YOU WANT?

To be condemned *in absentia* is to take the coward's way out of a threatening situation.

Missing a goal or making a major mistake has all the potential of being among life's better learning situations. Your superior is still like a father figure to you; his corrections may be severe, but you have every hope they will be just. Now is the time to follow his leadership as you never have before. Believe in him, trust his greater knowledge and experience, and benefit from his attempts to help you.

Remember one other point: your reaction when your employees avoid you. What suspicions flash through your mind when a man you are hunting is unaccountably missing from his work station? Why should he not be there when you have a legitimate point to check him out on? How much more does he know that you should be aware of and are not? If you follow your own thinking about this situation, you will understand what your superior is going through about you.

One more point should be kept in the forefront of your consciousness. If you have ever been guilty of avoiding your boss, be sure never to repeat that mistake. He will be permissive once or twice; don't expect him to let you go unquestioned for mistakes you may have made or are about to make. This is too much to expect of him, just as you should not be required to go that far with any of your people.

This discussion would be much too negative were we not to offer some suggestions for preventive maintenance. The most obvious one, and too ridiculous an oversimplification, would be to say that you make certain you never fall short of the mark. Suffice it to say that you are as human as the next supervisor, and that you will goof once in a while. The answer to this is mental and emotional maturity in the fullest sense of the words. Incurring a debt automatically obligates its payment, and the longer you put it off, the greater the interest charges that will accrue.

Do You Want More Responsibility?

The matter of responsibility becomes an all-governing element to the supervisor. He has deliberately chosen to take the heavier load; for this act, he is rewarded both financially and in prestige and position. He carries his load, and then some, because of the weight of responsibility he bears for the final outcome. This is the crux of his commitment to the company, and the reason why he is set apart from other employees.

Because of his choice, the supervisor has totally changed his way of life and altered his personal objectives. He has accepted a partial or total alienation of old friendships and associations as part of the sacrifice; he has cast his lot on the side of the company, and relaxes as best he can.

At this point, we are concerned with your capability of assuming heavier responsibilities in the near future. The determining factor will be your own sensitivity about the matter. How do you feel? Do you react in a strongly negative way to the concept of a heavier burden? Or do you have a potential reserve of strength which you feel responding to the challenge of the partially disclosed vista of lands to be conquered, and new areas to be explored? If this is your attitude, you are in an excellent position to go ahead with a development plan zeroed in on further advancement. Start immediately to map your strategy for the big move into middle management. Enlist every ally you can find, train your guns on the main target, and fire all batteries as long as your ammunition lasts.

How Burning Is Your Ambition?

Psychologists and physicians know that people vary widely in their tolerance to pain. We speak of high or low thresholds of pain. Analogously, people differ greatly in the amount of ambition they feel. Some very gifted men have never gone far because they felt no personal drive to better themselves. Others, with fewer natural endowments, have reached surprising heights on sheer grit and ambition. Any way you look at it, you will have to be deeply motivated to go upward in order to compensate for all the disadvantages experienced by occupants of the higher rungs of the organizational ladder.

Ambition may be a latent characteristic. It can lie dormant in a man for years, and then suddenly burst into a consuming flame when he is exposed to a particular stimulus which makes him avidly desire a different position. This man is called the late bloomer: He had the talents all the time, but had never been motivated to exercise them until quite late in life. Ambition is a trigger mechanism which unleashes formidable forces in any man. It can be touched off in many ways.

An overwhelming ambition in an ill-prepared man can be dangerous in the extreme. He will spin his wheels until completely frustrated; neuroses and even psychoses can be the result of this unfortunate circumstance. For that reason, no member of management should neglect the continuation of a tailored development plan as long as his basic personal ambitions are less than satisfied. If he has the tools, he can keep chipping away at the block of granite—the statue will finally emerge in all its glory, to the satisfaction of all his higher needs.

We have already indicated the saddest situation, the supervisor who has everything—except ambition. Now the other members of management are the ones to be frustrated, as they watch unrealized potential being wasted year after year. Carefully designed and artfully executed development plans are of little use here, for the central character is cold; there is no fire within him to assimilate and put into use the good things to which he is being exposed. If he reacts at all, and implements any of his newly acquired techniques, he will do so in the most perfunctory manner, with no verve or brilliance of execution.

How much ambition do you have at this point? Do you feel driven by unrequited needs to accomplish much more than you have so far? Do the heights above still beckon with the siren gesture, and inflame your imagination? You are the only person who can satisfactorily answer these questions, even though your answers will have a significant impact on the whole organizational structure. Your boss will be vitally interested in your answers, and so will his boss, and everyone in the chain of command above, clear to the top. Whether queried directly or not, you owe it to your superior to report from time to time your feelings in this area. Organizational planning is done at high levels and over long periods of time. Perhaps you think little of the importance of your situation to the structure at large, but the accumulation of your potential progress and that

HOW MUCH MORE RESPONSIBILITY DO YOU WANT?

of all other first-line supervisors is of crucial importance to the health of the enterprise. The mosaic can be seriously flawed by the absence of a single tiny piece.

In a major sense, ambition is totally blind to any other factor of your life. It takes no cognizance of your basic qualifications, or of the state of readiness for advancement in which you find yourself at the moment. If your sense of ambition is active, you will feel driven; if it is dormant, no other prod will make you react significantly.

The best practical approach to an assessment of the state of your ambition is an introspective examination of the pros and cons of further advancement. List what you consider the advantages and disadvantages of promotion, and cast up your own account. If the pluses are in a significant majority, there can be no question—you are obliged to bend your efforts toward another promotion. If the minuses outnumber the pluses, the answer is not quite so clear. If you are left confused and undecided, you could be feeling the first inkling of active ambition, which really doesn't give a rap about your arithmetic calculations. It will demand that you press on, regardless of whether the advantages and disadvantages balance out.

*   *   *

This chapter has been concerned with the extent to which you desire more responsibility. How are your nerves, on a day-to-day basis? Are you tense, irritable, jumpy? To what extent are you now forced to take work home with you several times a week, and would you be willing to take on an increased load in this area? What are your relationships with others at your level? Do your peers accept you, or do your contacts with them engender many enmities? How much delegation does your boss currently give you? Are you really allowed to operate as a supervisor, or does he delegate on a string? Are your relations with your boss free and easy, or do you frequently have to avoid him because of unmet commitments? Finally, how hot is your ambition—right now?

2

What Is the Job of the Middle Manager?

To be successful, a middle manager must choose one of two extremes. He can be totally resistant to change, thus perfectly maintaining the status quo, or he can be flexible enough to learn to live with almost any kind of change that can be thrown at him. The former alternative is much more difficult to accomplish. You will find it easier and more pragmatic to learn to roll with the punches and to live with innovation. You may perhaps feel that you do this to an extraordinary degree on your present job, but this characteristic in the job of the middle manager will be much more intense than anything you have experienced so far.

How Adaptable Are You—Right Now?

One good way to start to prepare yourself for this change in degree is to cultivate an awareness of new elements as they appear in your present environment, whether they are fortuitously introduced by outside random forces, or brought in by design by your own management. Once you have conditioned yourself to have an early sensitivity to the appearance of new things, you can train yourself to adjust to those which are not inimical to your work situation. The acceptance of change can become a habit, like any other human response to a stimulus. You must make a value judgment about the character of a specific change as a separate process; this judgment should not cloud your ability to adjust if necessary. Many times you will have to resign yourself to at least a temporary acceptance of something new, even though you know that you are prepared to wage a long fight to eradicate it. When you single-handedly take on a confrontation with something new, and refuse to build it into your life, you are in danger of bringing chaos into your work area, including serious impairment of your group's efficiency. You learned early in your experience as a supervisor that the work must go on at whatever cost. If you consider this hypocrisy, so be it. You will still have to go along with your management.

The truth of the saying that the best way to learn a thing is to teach it can be eminently demonstrated by observing how much you will learn about flexibility when you try to inculcate it in your people. They are the ones most seriously and personally affected by change, since it nearly always will result in new procedures in their operation. A series of changes implemented in a rigid work group can do immeasurable harm to group morale. Obviously, the best way to forestall this damage is to train your people to be flexible as a part of their natural job routine. As we said, you will be the one to benefit most by this process, because it will help you get ready for greater fluidity at the next level. If we accept greater change in the life of the middle manager, the implication is that he does not transmit down the line everything to which he is subjected. Many times his judgment will tell him that a proposed new idea would not be good for his area, and he will refuse to introduce it.

You should not infer from the above that all change in your work area will be engendered by your line. Your peers, who represent other work areas which have tangency with yours, will contribute a significant share of changes, either proposed or actual, in the way you conduct your business. Some of these will in fact be directly imposed upon you, such as new work standards generated by the industrial engineering department, or new procedures from the methods and systems section. You will probably have a greater tendency to resist changes from these sources than you will to resist those which have been sent down your line. Staff groups are notorious for their devilish ingenuity in gumming up the works for their peers. Even so, from your personal standpoint this is not always all bad, since it does give you practice in acquiring a viable method of meeting change.

The problem is to keep your sense of balance while you deal with all these variables. Unless you keep them in perspective, you may find yourself in a state of tension which will harm your personal worth as a supervisor, and strongly menace your chances for promotion. Your management will take a dim view of your going to pieces in the face of pressures, no matter what the cause. It is implicit in your job description that you will learn to live with stress and still remain functional at high levels of effectiveness. A good catharsis for the mental state which can arise from this situation is a probing of the scene with your superior, or with a good friend among your peers. Talking about the problem takes you a good way toward solving it. This means, of course, that you will be obliged to listen to your confidant when his pressures get to the boiling point. This give-and-take in a highly personal area is part of the ritual in the brotherhood of supervision.

The major consideration is that you deliberately set out to develop an ability to live with change on the job without seriously disturbing your mental balance. This goal is paramount if you are to have any hope for a quick promotion and an easy entrance into middle management. Your own superiors and your new peers will judge you heavily on your actions in this area, especially since your behavior under these pressures is clearly visible to all observers.

*Can You Implement Policy You Don't Make—
Every Time?*

When you become a middle manager, the first discovery you will probably make is that much of your time will be spent putting into force policy sent to you from your executive bosses. Policy is transformed into action at the center of the hierarchy. Procedures are either outlined or developed, and necessary communications are inaugurated to start the action down the line. One of the besetting sins

WHAT IS THE JOB OF THE MIDDLE MANAGER?

of middle management is the tendency to pass judgment on policies as they are generated. If consensus develops among the middle managers that a particular policy is not desirable, their concerted failure to act can completely vitiate that policy. This, on the face of it, is a betrayal of the trust of their superiors. The duty of the middle manager is clear: He has a perfect right to fight against a proposed policy before it has been adopted. Every argument he can bring to bear against it is legitimate, so long as the final decision has not been made. However, once the die has been cast, he is no longer in a position to question. Now his sole duty is to see that action is taken to support the new directive.

Middle managers resist new policy primarily because they see it as a threat to the status quo. No group of managers is more interested in a stable situation than are those at the center of the pyramid. They act as the fulcrum for the leverage of the entire organization. Stresses and strains on them during fundamental change are greater than those imposed on any other group of managers in the enterprise. The pressures they endure come from all directions—from executives above, from first-line supervisors below, and from peers on either side. In many cases, these pressures are opposable; the first line of management is dead set against a new policy because of results they anticipate in their work areas. Therefore, the middle manager truly finds himself at the center of a field of force of tremendous magnitude. He is often tempted to let a directive go by default rather than to be caught up in continuing strife.

The only acceptable answer to this dilemma is to reassert the fundamental responsibilities of the manager. There can be no excuse for his deliberate subversion of a considered policy sent down for him to implement. His character must be of sufficient strength to take this unpleasant development in stride and to carry through the necessary action. All this points up a common failing of executives: They are prone to believe that their duty is complete when they have drafted and communicated a directive. Many of them never follow through to see that it is activated down the line. For this reason, inaction at the point of their subordinates' sphere of influence can effectively reduce policy to impotence.

As a supervisor, you can put yourself into training for middle management by assuming a monitor's position for the procedures which are dropouts of new policy. You have the same responsibility here that your superior does for originating procedure to activate policy. In fact, in many cases it will be necessary for you to devise supplementary procedures to fit the special situation in your work area. When this happens, your overall efficiency will be measured by the sensitivity and speed of your response to this cue.

The experience of a large manufacturing company a few years ago can illustrate how far this kind of thing can be carried. The president and board of directors decided that it would be greatly advantageous to completely decentralize operations throughout the several divisions of the organization. The corporate vice-presidents realized immediately that their position would be at least cloudy, if not measurably weakened, by this change. They took a path of concerted inaction, and nearly six years elapsed before complete decentralization was effected. During this period, project managers, who theoretically were totally responsible for their part of the operation, were completely frustrated by corporate vice-presidents acting as if they were still responsible for the area. The ironic part of the story is that after the six years had elapsed, and the objective had finally been obtained, general conditions throughout the world, and particularly those within the industry, had changed to the point where a somewhat less complete recentralization movement had to be started. As might be suspected, managers at all levels exhibited considerable confusion and cynicism. They were quite vocal in questioning whether the executive echelon really knew where they wanted to go, or whether their basic managerial decisions were whimsical. Oddly enough, there was no question in either of the basic changes about any lack of communication up and down the line. Announcements were clear, lucid, and definitive. The blockage and heel dragging were purely the reactions of managers who thought their position and power were being threatened.

This situation is not unique. It is repeated in kind and degree many times every year in American industry. Members of management finding themselves in fundamental change actually have no alternative if they are to discharge their managerial duties effectively. If they find it impossible to do so, their only honorable recourse is to resign. The present proliferation of mergers and acquisitions often increases the number of traumatic managerial dilemmas. The new corporate ownership might well have a philosophy directly opposite to the old one. This means that new and different policies will be immediately forthcoming, and sometimes represents such major changes that managers find them impossible to accept. In recent years, this occurrence has contributed hugely to managerial turnover in business and industry. It reinforces the dictum already stated: If your basic principles are attacked, you will find it impossible to go on.

Are Your Conceptual Skills Healthy?

When you were inducted into the ranks of supervision, it was indicated to you in one way or another that you were not expected to spend too much time in conceptualizing on your job. Second- and third-line managers feel uncomfortable in the presence of a first-line supervisor who shows a deep knowledge of the entire business and perhaps even of the industry. Moreover, a supervisor who is skillful at viewing the whole picture is also likely to be innovative, and this leads to upsets in his work area. From the standpoint of orderly production on a day-to-day basis, it is better not to show too much imagination. The philosophy of a large percentage of the lower strata of management is to let the changes filter down from the top.

However, there can be little doubt that those members of middle and upper management who agreed to your promotion scanned your ability to conceptualize as one of the skills which could make you more promotable. As a middle manager, you must begin to use conceptual skills in your job, since you will be managing different units doing different work. It will be up to you to weld these bits and pieces into a unified whole which can perform harmoniously and profitably.

The fact that you will not be strongly encouraged to paint with a broad brush (unless your boss is taking a truly personal interest in your advancement) does not mean that you have no freedom of action in learning more about your business. You can do this on your own, and quietly, so that no managers will become upset or feel any threat from your actions. In most cases, the records are there for anyone to use to find out what is going on. Your financial people, your sales personnel, your procurement personnel, your industrial relations sections—all will be glad to provide you access to the records when you can show a need to know, and usually this is not necessary.

During the past few years, one of the richer veins for the conceptualizer has been the study of organizational structure. In many businesses, new methods have been grafted onto old organizations with no attempt to determine whether changes in the organization would make the new methods work more efficiently and profitably. One reason for this lack of study has been inertia generated by a fear that the new methods will result in a reduction in force. A prime example of this has been the attitude of many managers (and workers) toward electronic data processing. Many actually dreaded the coming of the computer because they envisioned it as the axe which would lop off large numbers of jobs. To date, these fears have proved unjustified. In most businesses the installation of a computer has resulted in an increase in total employment, although some of the old jobs were eliminated. Nevertheless, whenever any new method or system is installed, a long hard look should be taken to be sure that the organizational structure is still functional, and capable of getting the best results from the innovation. As an interested observer, you are in a better position to see possible improvements in structure than is the man who first formed them and probably still feels a pride of authorship in them.

As for your knowledge of the rest of the industry, most

businesses of any size belong to trade associations or professional groups dealing with the business in which your company is engaged. A major duty of these groups is to keep industry data and statistics. They also report immediately new developments of significance, and they disseminate news to all interested parties. Most of this information will be in the hands of someone in your business, and you will have access to it at no cost. Some homework will pay well here.

Do You Keep Good Records?

Mere possession of large amounts of information about your business will not ensure the development of your conceptual skills. You must put the information to work in new combinations so that you will stand apart from the crowd. Now is the time to build your armory for use when you become a middle manager. Keep good records, especially of any ways you see to improve the operation in your line of progression. Some of these ideas might be welcomed by your management right now; others should be deferred until you have more latitude of movement and authority. If you enter middle management with a battery of backup plans, you will be much more likely to get off to a running start in your new job.

How Are Your Interdepartmental Relationships?

Organizational structure, of course, is only one of the areas you might want to explore with an eye to planning for constructive change. Another which you should work much harder on is the matter of liaison with other departments. As the work of all managers becomes more complex every day, the importance of these lateral relationships increases. Anything which can be done to simplify and make more functional these interdepartmental relationships can only result in great good for the enterprise.

Whatever your point of attack may be, a serious effort to develop your conceptual skills will strengthen your chances for promotion into middle management. This is a very personal procedure. Others may help with suggestions and designs of training methods, but the real learning process must be yours alone. If you read your general climate as not too sympathetic to this exercise, you can still make real progress without the knowledge of others. The basic tools—that is, the body of information you need—should concern only you. You have every right as a practicing supervisor to acquire this knowledge, for use now or in the future. At the same time, this activity will result in benefits to your present job. You will find useful methods which can save you work and money where you are right now.

How Well Do You Delegate?

The question of your ability to delegate will take on more meaning when you are promoted again. For a long time you have been accustomed to delegating small pieces of the action to hourly workers on the line or to general salaried personnel in the office. You may have occupied a lead position for some time before you were made a supervisor. Under these circumstances, you developed a style of delegation peculiar to your own personality and how you related to the personalities of your subordinates. In any event, the delegation has usually been fairly clear, terse, and directive. This is the manner most commonly used where the work is done—mostly because of the intolerable pressures of time. The man who is making the product or performing the service and his immediate superior simply do not have the time to be as polite as they are in normal social interactions. Furthermore, many employees would neither understand nor respect a superior who suggested rather than directed. Part of this is not necessarily a reaction to a more sophisticated managerial style; rather, it is an indication of a growing feeling of insecurity arising from a looser and less definitive kind of delegation.

On the other hand, when you come to managing other managers, your first instinct (and the right one) is to take a more formal approach to your subordinate managers. Most of them will fiercely resent your giving them a direct order. Among managers, this technique is almost never used unless there has been an indication of incipient insubordination; in that situation, the direct order has every feature of an open threat from the superior. If your subordinate manager has enough on the ball to succeed, he is going to know that your suggestions and requests are every bit as much orders as if they had been couched as absolute directives. By using these forms, however, you are supporting his ego and allowing him to look good before his people.

Another factor to consider immediately upon your promotion to the second level is that you may have insecurity symptoms of your own about your ability to manage other managers. A quite natural reaction to this fear is to keep the reins in your own hands, and to try to do all the work yourself. Although this is as absurd as it sounds, it is a human reaction to a new and strange situation. Any manager knows that it is a spiritual, mental, and physical impossibility to be three, four, or five first-line supervisors simultaneously. In your own immediate past you have ample evidence of how difficult it is to do justice to one area. *The only reasonable answer is to delegate—and delegate properly.*

You must have trust and confidence enough in your subordinates to anticipate their doing an adequate or better job of first-line supervision, just as your superior had in you when you first became a management employee. This does not for one minute suggest that you should fail to establish controls or to follow up to see that the work is being done properly. What it does mean is that you can't do it all yourself. The proper division of labor is the primary reason for designing an organizational structure.

There is another psychological implication of your demonstrating good delegation to your subordinates. People instinctively respond to a given kind of approach in a like manner. If you treat your subordinates as mature, responsible adults, the majority of them will respond as such. The fact that you are showing confidence in them will elicit their best efforts to show that they are worthy of your trust. Nobody likes to fail a test which is given to him openly and confidently.

The major criterion for successful delegation is the timing and number of controls instituted. One of the curses of American industry is the veritable deluge of useless paperwork generated by ill-planned controls which are functional for no one. Not all subordinates necessarily should respond with identical frequency to any control. People work differently, with different degrees of accuracy, and with varying feelings of responsibility. Why should not their superior recognize these individual differences and set up his controls accordingly? For example, some people perform brilliantly when required to report once a month. Others should be asked for an accounting on a weekly basis, and there are those who work best when keeping daily logs and reporting at the end of each shift. You, as the superior, will have the duty of determining to your own satisfaction the frequency and number of controls instituted for your subordinates. Your guideline should be, of course, what is most functional and efficient for your part of the organization's activity. Certainly, as the man in charge, you have the authority to establish these conditions, and can experiment for a reasonable amount of time to determine optimal conditions of delegation. Everyone concerned will be happier under this working arrangement, and the net result, as indicated, will be a significant reduction in paperwork. This in itself will be a major gain for your total operation.

The amount of delegation existing within a department is a good barometer of the mental and emotional maturity of its supervision. Even in a strongly centralized form of operation, clearly defined limits of delegation must be established and communicated up and down the line. Of course, in a decentralized operation, this is the premise on which the enterprise rests—total delegation to the lowest possible point in the structure.

WHAT IS THE JOB OF THE MIDDLE MANAGER?

Can You Manage New Disciplines?

Almost every middle manager has under his direction more than one discipline, or more than one function of the enterprise. That is, a manager might be promoted into an area where he will be expected to have reporting to him workers in a field with which he is not familiar. This situation poses a threat to most men the first time they meet it. They have been so used to having expertise in the technical end of the work they manage that their lack of experience in a part of the new situation frightens them. There are two principal approaches to this problem—or three, if you consider a combination of the two.

The first method is to make a Herculean effort to get necessary basic knowledge overnight. While this technique offers definite advantages in reducing your anxiety to a reasonable level, it is not functional in making you capable of holding your own when discussing technical problems. So long as you remember this, and evade efforts of others to involve you as referee in these problems, you can, by diligent effort, quickly become proficient in the new area. The simple process of continued immersion in the discipline will hasten the learning process.

The second method is to hire, and rely upon, technical people as personal staff to take care of the problem. This is a viable procedure, as long as you have absolute trust and confidence in the knowledge and judgment of your technical staff. Under this system, you will, at least for a time, of necessity delegate to them a significant part of your decision making in technical matters. This is an uncomfortable position for most managers, especially when they are new and somewhat insecure in their position. However, it will obviate the possibility of being trapped into making decisions in areas where you are less than perfectly qualified. The one fatal error possible in this situation would be to continue delegating to technical staff parts of your job for which *they* are not qualified. This would amount to nothing less than abdication of your job, and is not defensible.

The third approach is to make reasonably heavy demands upon your time and attention in gaining necessary new knowledge, *and* to hire technical staff. Under this arrangement, the staff personnel would quickly fit into a consultative position, they would give you advice, and you would make your own decisions. Of the three methods described, the last is ordinarily most satisfying to the manager's ego and morale. You are not forced to lose face with the rest of your subordinates, and they will quickly identify with your group and recognize you as the leader.

Can You Coordinate the Work of Your Subordinates?

There is much more to your new job than the necessity of becoming familiar with new fields. Your subordinates must be welded into a functional, working team. Often, they will exhibit strong rivalries—even jealousies—in their interactions. This is quite natural. Your job as their manager is to channel their energies in constructive directions, rather than allowing these rivalries to endanger your whole organization. The middle manager needs human skills as much as the first-line supervisor does. He finds his cues to be more subtle, and he doubtless wants to use different approaches to subordinates from those he used as a first-line supervisor. However, the basic psychological principles are the same, and his need to apply them has not diminished.

One of the visible goals of your job as a middle manager is to train your subordinates in their coordinating activities toward a smooth total operation. The implications of this objective will include their becoming sophisticated about what their peers are doing. The amount of ignorance in this area is truly appalling. It is possible for five or six subordinate managers to see each other daily, to sit together frequently in staff meetings, and theoretically to be working toward the same group goals, and yet all the time not really know what the jobs of the other managers are. As their leader, your responsibility is to overcome this problem. It takes a positive stimulus on your part to get any reaction from them. It is only too human for each of us to become so absorbed in the problems and activities of our own group that we have no time to think of what others are doing. This must be changed, and quickly.

Your objectives as a middle manager can never be realized until your subordinates cooperate fully on a basis of at least a minimal common knowledge of what all their peers are doing and are responsible for. On-the-job training will have to be devised and administered as your personal responsibility. If any delegation is involved, you will be responsible for close control and continuing follow-up. One of the more obvious of the usable methods is to require regular reports in staff meetings from a given member of the overall activity. A major part of each staff meeting can justifiably be allocated to this procedure. If you indicate clearly that you are monitoring these reports closely, the personnel involved will soon do them well. Competition will increase the interest and attention of the other members.

This accomplishment will be no small part of your settling into a new job as a middle manager. Its importance to your total success is so great that any amount of effort and ingenuity you expend is justified. This one aspect can make or break you as a middle manager.

What's Your Coordination Factor?

We mentioned briefly how important it is for a manager to be able to work effectively with those over whom he has no line authority. As you enter middle management, this matter of liaison or coordination will loom several times larger than ever before. From here on out, you will do more and more of your work interdepartmentally, and the key to your success will be your ability as a coordinator. Anyone performing this function is analogous to a chemical catalyst—an agent which increases the speed and amount of a chemical reaction without being itself permanently altered. The coordinator must keep in balance an infinite number of details, must see that things happen on time, and must be sure that those involved relate to each other in reasonable harmony. As you might guess from this definition, coordination is a job of no mean proportions. To be a good coordinator, a manager must be willing to efface his own personality. He must have exceptional powers in interpersonal relationships and, above everything else, he must remain calm under any difficulty or sudden emergency.

WHAT IS THE JOB OF THE MIDDLE MANAGER?

It is obvious from this description that the manager's communicative abilities must be exceptional, both orally and in writing. One training director who was widely known throughout the industry and within his professional group for being unusually proficient in coordination had a fault which nearly proved his downfall time after time. He could weave the most intricate network of communications among managers to perfection concerning a given event or process. Timing, arrangements, interfaces between several disciplines, logistics—all were impeccable and a joy to behold. The one tragic factor was that he was nearly certain to forget to tie his secretary in with one or two key steps in the intricate proceedings. Needless to say, this omission could scuttle the whole scheme.

Happily, the art of coordination is eminently learnable. Detailed and complicated as it may sometimes be, everything about it is amenable to rather simple training operations. Expertise in this area can be acquired by sheer concentration and adequate record keeping. The latter is the answer to the whole thing. Tickler files, cross-references, and check sheets are the keys. If you set up a master plan in advance with attention to detail, and then follow it meticulously, you can gain an enviable reputation as a coordinator.

Lest we be guilty of oversimplification, we should recognize the importance of the high order of cooperation required by all concerned for a group effort to be brought to a successful conclusion. Here the coordinator starts to act like the catalyst. His sensitivity must be great enough to alert him to possible communications breakdowns, or to the development of abrasive reactions between two of the respondents. When these occur, the good coordinator goes into action smoothly, calmly, and quietly. He sees that the logjams are broken, and that ruffled feelings are soothed without loss of face for either party. Once you have achieved the virtuoso rating as a coordinator, you will be able to fit these individual pieces into the pattern without breaking or badly bending any of them.

To win a good reputation as a coordinator, you will find it necessary to depend heavily on your team of subordinates. The networks become extremely complex, and details can run into the scores, and hundreds, in some big operations. Naturally, you will have to delegate much of the detail work to several of the people reporting to you. This implies rigorous formal or on-the-job training of your staff, which is, of course, a desirable end in itself.

This one talent can make or break a man desirous of advancement into middle management. If you want to aid in the development of your subordinates, you will not hesitate to spend a considerable amount of time helping them to become competent coordinators. This is one area in which good progress is quickly visible and quickly rewarded. Give them a modicum of training, choose exactly the right vehicle, and turn them loose with assurances of your complete confidence in their ability to do the job to their credit and yours.

The matter of coordination, vital as it obviously is, has been strangely neglected in management literature. Few references are made to either the techniques or theory of this extremely important facet in the life of the middle manager. To all intents and purposes, you are pretty much on your own, and you will be required to be your own resource in helping both yourself and your people to become proficient coordinators.

*   *   *

This chapter has delineated (somewhat by indirection) the nature of your job as a middle manager. You must be greatly adaptable, since you will be subjected to tremendous pressures from all directions. Much of your work will be in the implementation of policy which you will not make. At this level you will be required to use whatever conceptual skills you have, and to develop them assiduously. Your need to be good at delegation will increase noticeably when you enter middle management, especially since you will probably be learning one or more new disciplines yourself. Finally, you will be called upon to spend a significant amount of your time in the job of coordination.

3

How Do You Manage Other Managers?

A lot of talking is done about the change that occurs in the management job when the subordinates are other managers instead of hourly workers or general salaried personnel. In fact, an aura of strangeness sometimes arises about the middle manager's job because so much emphasis is placed on this difference.

Are Managers Really Different?

To keep our perspective, we must try to determine whether a manager actually differs that much from other people. First of all, the inescapable fact is that they are human beings. Therefore, fundamental and common psychological factors are operative in both managers and other people. All of us respond to basic stimuli in a predictable manner, according to our individual characteristics. Each of us has his own way of perceiving a threat and reacting to protect himself from it.

In some areas, a person attracted to management will behave differently from a person who is not. First, he will have identified on the side of the company finally and irrevocably. This decision is the basic rock on which his entire career will be built. If he ever feels serious doubt about this commitment, he is in the wrong business. This commitment is highest on his list of priorities, and it will affect many of his personal actions throughout his life. For example, he may agree to move from the part of the country in which he was born and raised, and for which he has a deep feeling. Making this choice will have a far-reaching impact on other members of his family who are not as strongly committed to the enterprise.

Secondly, the motivation of the manager differs from that of the line worker, in both kind and degree. It is common for the manager to work hard to achieve power or status, or both. He finds in the management position more chances to achieve these objectives than he does as a salaried employee or an hourly worker. Having chosen this avenue toward an attractive goal, his actions in management will be predictable in many situations. For example, his power drive will embroil him in company politics much more quickly and deeply than a person not so fascinated by power. Similarly, if status is a major goal, he may spend an inordinate amount of time and energy assuring himself of as high a position on the totem pole as he can possibly achieve.

More and more in modern management, the successful candidate for promotion is going to have to be more perceptive, and to have more empathy, in the area of human skills. His people are much more independent, both financially and socially, than they were a generation ago. Their reactions to what they consider undesirable surroundings will be quick and sharp. This means that the boss will have to adapt his behavior to situations which a manager of the last generation would not have recognized.

The manager's deeper-than-average commitment to the organization will result in greater dedication to his work. He will recognize many things which have to be done, no matter how much of his personal time they require. It is a common sight to see the manager carrying his briefcase almost everywhere he goes; his workweek will be nearly double what it was before he entered management. If he is a true manager, this extra effort will not bother him, since he will experience a great deal of personal satisfaction in his accomplishments.

Another obvious difference between the manager and others is that he must have at least the elements of leadership within him, whether trained and functional, or merely rough and unpolished. He is inner directed to the point of demanding to make many decisions for himself, whereas the follower is afraid of being put into the decision-making situation. The manager has adjusted personally to the fact that he is a member of the minority, and always will be. Whatever reinforcement he finds necessary will be provided by his interaction with his peers and with those above him in the hierarchy. He is not afraid of being forced to be a loner.

Oddly enough, in order to operate successfully with only his own resources, he must have a much broader view of the whole picture than does a follower. This comes from having to make many comparisons and choices during his day-to-day business activities. This honing of his judgmental ability must be done in connection with both people and things. The individual contributor may be able to go through his working life completely centered on things; the manager can never do this. In fact, as he rises through the steps of the hierarchy, he will become oriented more and more toward people, and will depend on hired technical expertise for decisions about things.

It would be wrong to assume from the above that there is less room for individual differences among managerial personnel than there is among their followers. We are simply pointing out some of the characteristics common to successful managers wherever they are found. The gist is this: The middle manager will recognize a small group of differences in the subordinates he now has when he compares them to those he supervised when he was at the first line. This understanding will alter his managerial job in fundamental aspects, and will change his approach to the common problems of all supervision.

How Do You Resolve Conflict Among Subordinates?

When you enter middle management, you will at once observe one difference among your subordinates. The competition in the group will be much more keen and continuous than it was when you were supervising at the first line. Most of the managers you now have under you will be ambitious, keen, and ready to take advantage of the situation whenever possible. You can expect considerable conflict, both overt and hidden, among your subordinates. Your responsibility as leader will demand that you exercise a close control over this conflict for the good of the order and the effectiveness of your group.

If we choose to follow the nomenclature and conceptualization of Blake and Mouton and their Managerial Grid, we are concerned with the differences in the approach to conflict of the five principal managerial styles. The 9.1 manager has little tolerance for conflict within his group. He sees it as a threat to his control, and will take quick action (generally rough) to subdue it. He believes that conflict among the crew can only result in lowered production, which is anathema to him.

The 1.9 (country club) manager is terrified at the sign of conflict, since it indicates trouble in his big happy family. His reaction to conflict is to give away the store in an effort to placate the grievances of his people. In the long run, as soon as his subordinates realize they can have almost anything they ask for, his life will become more and more complicated every day. Their requests will get increasingly outrageous with every failure of his to stand firm. Over an extended period the 1.9 position is untenable, and must be abandoned.

The 1.1 (great gray abdicator) will refuse to face conflict at all. His reaction is either to fail to recognize its presence, or simply to disappear and let things take their course. Any serious conflict in this manager's organization will cause it to be torn apart.

The 5.5 position epitomizes the style which is viable for most middle managers most of the time. Subjected as you are to pressures from above, below, and all sides, the word for the 5.5 manager is "compromise." In this attitude you will be disturbed by the possible consequences of continued conflict among your subordinates, but you will recognize your responsibility to do something about it. Compromise has the advantage of not allowing anyone to become a total loser; neither will anyone win. Everyone saves face, and it is easier to resolve hurt feelings if everyone gets part of what he wanted.

You will be a typical member of middle management if you adopt this managerial style when you perceive that two of your subordinates are seriously at odds. It is questionable, however, how much valuable training and developmental experiences you are giving your subordinates by adopting this procedure. The deepest and most meaningful learning ever undergone is associated with blatant failures and conspicuous successes. If you are serious about wanting to bring along the managers in your group, you might consider taking the 9.9 attitude.

The only difficulty with the last statement is that few managers have enough autonomy to operate in this style more than infrequently. The basic assumption of the 9.9 position is that the manager has nearly complete control of the operations within his group. When this is possible, the word for the 9.9 manager is "confrontation." In effect, when he sees conflict developing among his men, he keeps hands off and, in essence, urges them to fight it out to a finish. Somebody will win, and somebody will lose. There will be a clean-cut and definitive resolution of the problem. As already indicated, this is a fertile field for individual growth and development. As the members of the managerial team go through a succession of conflict situations, they learn much about management as a field, decision making, interpersonal relationships, and a proper conceptualization of their job. It is a hard school, but a good one.

These five possible attitudes toward conflict among subordinates cover a fairly large number of possibilities. Your choice of an approach will have to be governed by your knowledge of yourself and your people, plus your own estimation of other independent variables. It would be disastrous to assume that you could use only one of these managerial styles and invoke it every time conflict arose. Things and people both will change over a period of time. Your job is always to remain alert enough to evaluate the situation and to take whatever action you deem appropriate.

In the final analysis, you should be extremely worried if you never observe conflict developing among your subordinates. This would be an indication of a moribund organization. If there is life and growth within your group, there will be differences of opinion, and there will be struggles for power and position. Hopefully, there will never be too long a time between eruptions of conflict within your group. However, if your general treatment of them is thought of as a learning situation, you can both remove much of the sting of abrasive personalities, and make some good departmental decisions. Not the least of the values to be derived is help in making up your mind about the comparative potential of the people working for you. Anyone can look good when he has no problems; the man headed for the top is the one who can handle himself well when under attack.

How Do You React to the Jealous Subordinate?

It is quite common to oversimplify—to say that an adult who shows jealousy is emotionally immature. We shrug it off, as if this were an answer to the problem, rather than a statement about it. Of course the jealous adult is emotionally childlike in this respect, but what if he is otherwise a valuable and productive employee, and ordinarily a better-than-average supervisor? Would you allow this one fault to wash him out, and thereby lose his potential to the group?

Before making any dangerous generalizations of possible cures for this malady, we should clarify various kinds of jealousies, and to what degree they are shown. From your standpoint as a manager and superior, you are really concerned much more with jealousies among your subordinates than you are with those directed at you. Any man worthy of being brought along for better things will be shooting for your job. You wouldn't think much of him if he weren't. If you personify the obstacles to his ambitions, and this takes the form of jealousy, what could be more human and natural? Then again, how often does this employee exhibit his emotion visibly? Once or twice a year? A couple of times a month? Several times a week? Why not get some kind of reading on the depth and extent of his emotion before you plan and implement corrective action?

In all fairness to the man, you must also double-check

to be sure that he has no realistic reason for his jealousy. Have you given him every opportunity for self-development and growth? Does he get his share of chances to do the unusually good job? Is the division of labor—and the chance for recognition—truly fair throughout the organization? Look hard now: What possible reasons may he have for thinking he has been unfairly treated? Are you sure you're sure?

What Treatment Do You Use?

Once some of these interpersonal assessments have been accomplished, you can begin to think in terms of treatment. Direct counseling about the problem is probably contraindicated—at least at first. A prima-donna reaction such as jealousy of the superior is not easily amenable to the logical approach needed in personal counseling. There is great likelihood that such counseling, if used at the outset, will only compound the difficulties. Better to approach him from the blind side by reinforcing in every visible way you can the objectivity of your treatment of subordinates. Review company and departmental policy on employee relations in your staff meetings once in a while. Demonstrate incontrovertibly that the way you split up responsibilities among your people is fair and equitable. After a reasonable concentration of such therapeutic actions, your subordinate, if normally acute, will be better conditioned to sit down with you and have a long, open chat on the state of your relationship on the job.

More important to you than the above is that case when your man indulges himself in petty jealousies of his peers.

This situation, if not quickly checked, can be a prime disrupter of organizations. Normally, the first reaction of others to known jealousies will be amusement, then irritation, and quickly thereafter, reprisal tactics. Moreover, polarization often follows, as friends of both parties become embroiled in the activity, and array themselves on the two sides of the quarrel. Many full-scale organizational battles have resulted from the exhibition of small jealousies between two individuals. Such conflicts can be blown up into threats of formidable proportions.

You will experience few more rigorous tests of your objectivity and qualities of leadership than in this situation. It is obvious to you at once that firm action will be required on your part, but the big question remains: against whom or what, and of what nature?

Basically, you are faced with a retraining job of your group in their interpersonal relationships, especially as they affect the performance of the group. Most of the people will respond positively to significant evidence that the effectiveness of your organization is being changed, and will regain their perspective quickly. But you may not have smoothed the feathers of the original culprit—the jealous subordinate. He will probably take some special handling and a little extra effort. You, Mr. Middle Manager, face one of the unique challenges to your ingenuity and inventiveness.

Our constantly increasing absorption with status has its origin in personal jealousies. Actually, the amount of work which rolls across a manager's desk should not be affected by whether that desk is made of metal or mahogany, and has one pedestal or two. Yet, many of us are venal enough to be irritated when a rival winds up with the choice office, or the next available company membership in the country club.

Another observation is in order here. The manager who has time to indulge himself in jealousies is probably not being stretched enough on the job. Maybe some of the challenge has gone; perhaps he should reexamine his personal goals and objectives. One attack on the problem should be tried soon: Hold an unscheduled performance review, and renegotiate your man's performance standards to be sure they are high enough to make him reach. The latent narcissism revealed by personal jealousies is often subdued by making the job more demanding. You cannot manipulate a subordinate into happiness or a general state of euphoria, but you can make sure that he doesn't have free time on the job to indulge in misguided introspection leading down the primrose path. A warning to you, the superior: Don't let the natural irritation inherent in this situation twist you out of shape. Don't overreact to an annoyance which should remain nothing more than that, and thereby risk the general health of your organization.

Are You Ready for Management by Objectives?

If you are not already doing so, within the next few years, you will have to be able to operate within a system called Management by Objectives, or MBO, in order to remain in management. Under this system, goals for a specified increment of time are negotiated between superior and subordinate, and managerial performance is then measured against achievement below, at the level of, or above the standards already set. The theory is logical and defensible. By this method, a large part of the obtrusive subjectivity is removed, and the two principals can achieve a much better meeting of the minds. The entire cyclical process results in much less trauma and a lower anxiety level for both members of the team. When we operate against established bench marks, we do not feel personally threatened, as we do when the measures are not clearly understood, or are totally unknown.

Some factors in Management by Objectives make a transition from the traditional seat-of-the-pants management difficult to achieve. First, all suspicion of the motivation of the superior must be removed. It is his job to convince you that he is sincere in wanting to improve both your and his managerial performance on measured increments. This is especially difficult, since it also requires your superior to convince himself that this *is* the case. There is, unfortunately, a certain amount of personal security in being able to rate a subordinate's performance by means of the crystal ball. That is, he cannot demand you to defend your position. You have spoken, and that is that.

The second factor is that it is hard to agree on objectives the first time or so around the cycle. The tendency is for the subordinate to set his goals unreasonably high, and for the supervisor to set them insultingly low. Once the goals are established, it takes some doing for the two parties to compromise gracefully. This must be done to get the system off the ground.

Third, you will be hampered in these first involvements by lack of historical data to serve as points of reference. Your standards will be pulled out of the hat, and will be significantly off the mark in most cases. So long as you expect this, and can live with it, the difficulty will not be insurmountable. The second and third cycles can be much more closely drawn and will therefore be more functional. By this time, you will have involved your people in the process, and will be getting feedback from them which can serve as guideposts for establishing your next objectives.

Finally, this new approach will entail changing some deep-rooted work habits. Your entire focus must be shifted from a general survey to a pinpointing of four or five major objectives for each time period. These goals will also come and go as emphasis shifts from one weak spot to another. We all know how hard it is for an adult to change his habits, especially when the desired new one is almost the reverse of the one he wants to eradicate. There is no better time to elicit the utmost in cooperation and goodwill from every member of your team.

We have described the general contour of the battle; now perhaps we should indicate the reason for the war. There can be little doubt that Management by Objectives will emerge in the future as a universal *modus operandi* for American business and industry. This means that any manager desirous of remaining competitive will have to play the game. Therefore, a general retraining of all personnel within your group will be necessary. Nothing can be gained if your boss and you decide upon this procedure unless you call in the troops, explain the new ground rules to them, and solicit their help. Management by Objectives is definitely a group project, a group way of life. Forget it, unless you can get everyone going your way.

Few exercises in management will demand more expertise in all the managerial functions than this one. Your planning must be meticulous and complete. You must provide for every contingency, and have an answer ready for every question—limitless as the number may seem at first. To be salable, the package you present to your people must be unassailable in logic and orderliness. They must be able to see what is in it for them if they are to make a full commitment and identification.

The organizational aspects may entail a shifting of major responsibilities almost at random. Never before will you have found it quite so necessary to fit job responsibilities to the personalities and capabilities of the people in your group. The necessity of working as a team becomes overpowering. Unless every member exerts his utmost to contribute, coordinate, and cooperate, you will already have failed. This, too, must be communicated to all your people completely and fully, with no punches pulled.

Your method of direction will change in all essential details. The onus of performance is going to be shifted directly to each individual concerned. "The buck stops here," as the sign on President Truman's desk said. Since everyone will have his own personal goals and performance standards, your requirements for leadership will be personalized to the final degree. There will be no more necessity for general directives or policy clarifications. At least, this is a clear net gain for all.

Controls will, of course, be completely rewritten, since their reason for being has been shifted from directive to permissive orientation. They now represent the medium for the collection of data, rather than booby traps for the unwary adventurer. Your sole purpose is to track your progress toward your group's objectives; nothing personal is involved, and no recriminations are to be expected. Long live Management by Objectives if it achieves these organizational objectives.

How Are Managers Motivated?

To say that managers are motivated by the same goals as any other human being would be the truth, but not the whole truth. Studies have shown that managers, as a population, tend to be more strongly motivated than most people by three factors: money, power, and prestige. Of the three, money is the most dangerous motivator for the middle manager to control for his subordinates.

Money as a motivator has a different effect on managers from its effect on most people. There is always an element of comparison in the employee's mind when he thinks of the money he is being paid. The first consideration is whether his pay is adequate for the job he is doing and the contribution he is making. In most cases, a good manager is quite objective in approaching this judgment. He knows his own capacity; he knows the parameters of the job; he knows the strengths and weaknesses of his peers. By the time a manager has risen to the middle areas of his hierarchy, he is making enough money so that his material needs are eminently well satisfied. More often than not, he may be faced with the fact that another promotion will put him into a new tax bracket where his net income may be next to nothing. Yet he will fight grimly with everything in him to get that promotion for the psychic satisfaction of achieving the goal. Money has become a symbol rather than an actuality, and men will devote their whole being to its pursuit.

You as a middle manager can effectively use money as a motivator with your subordinates. The best method is to operate within the framework of a well-designed and well-communicated wage and salary policy. The possibility of upward movement should be clearly designated within each salary grade. Then, exceptional performance can be rewarded in a concrete, irrefutable manner. A merit raise under this system is another medal which your subordinate will treasure.

Power drive exhibits itself in many ways. One of the most common is the interest a person evinces into getting into management. Almost everyone perceives the manager as a person who possesses a significant amount of power; therefore, the managerial position becomes highly desirable to those who value power. This is not to say that everyone will use power in the same way, once it is achieved. Each of us uses power according to the dictates of his basic character and personality. Therefore, you must have a deep knowledge of each of your people as an individual, and develop the ability to predict how each will react to the possession of power. In fact, this judgment of yours should be a separator when you start considering advancements and promotions. You may decide that one of your men is simply not yet mature enough to be advanced. You fear that he might react negatively to a sudden increase in power. Your responsibility then is to give him as much help as you can to mature to the point where he can tolerate more power and use it wisely.

This negative decision about a subordinate's immediate promotion should never be considered as final. Remember that chronological age has only a small correlation with emotional maturity—hardly enough to be significant, in fact. A person of any age can continue to mature emotionally, and eventually to be capable of taking on more responsibility successfully. Since managerial power reaches into all facets of the organization, and affects money, men, and materials, the answer to this problem is obvious: Help the subordinate to widen his perspective and to deepen his experience in all parts of his job in order to achieve the desired maturity. Making this possible will be your responsibility.

The consideration of prestige (or status) as a managerial motivator has some subtle implications for you as a middle manager. Prestige has two distinct aspects: that which is in the eye of the beholder, and that which is intrinsic and implicit in the position itself. The two are seldom equated on a one-to-one basis. This fact is well illustrated in the matter of job titles. In most industrial organizations, a vice-president has considerable power and prestige. He will surely be at the policy-making level, with influence of no mean proportions in many functions other than his own. On the other hand, traditionally, a vice-president in a bank may not even be at the middle management level, let alone be a policy maker. His prestige (and power) are strictly limited, and he makes decisions within a closely circumscribed range.

The other side of the coin is that many jobs become prestigious as a result of what the incumbent does with them. His actions, his evidence of managerial know-how, and his skill in weaving a strong web of peer relationships may increase the status of the job far beyond what its position on the organization chart would indicate to the casual observer. When this happens, we know we are watching a manager who has great potential and who will go still higher up the ladder.

You, as a middle manager, have more than a little control over the amount of prestige inherent in the jobs your subordinates hold. As their leader, you can elevate or lower the status of any of your people at will. We are assuming that you will not be guilty of a venal manipulation of prestige; your intent must be to use job prestige in a benign manner as a managerial motivator. When you work in these areas you are dealing with strong stuff, and it is incumbent upon you, the manager, to be objective and impartial at all times.

Can You Really Be Objective About Subordinates?

We do much talking and writing in managerial circles about the necessity for being objective in our considerations of subordinates. The question remains: Is this a possibility, or only a goal toward which we must constantly work? To ask any man to eradicate all personal reactions in thinking about another human being is to demand that he be more than human himself. Whether or not we care to admit it, our likes and dislikes color our thinking and warp our judgment. Your chore as a manager, then, is to reduce this subjectivity to the lowest possible point, and to examine yourself continuously for evidences of prejudice. This activity is especially necessary in your interactions with subordinates on the job.

When approaching a decision which involves the future of one of your people, you can best assure the most nearly dispassionate attitude by discussing the matter with the man concerned. The important guideposts, if mutually agreed upon, will be free from negative influences exerted by the thinking of either one. This means that you must arrive at your decision during the discussion, but you can cut away most of the deadwood which could otherwise obscure your vision of the desired goal. As a manager of managers, your relationship with your subordinates will undergo some slight but significant changes. Little by little, elements of the colleague relationship will creep in. You will ordinarily give your people more latitude in decision making within their area of responsibility, and your controls will become less restrictive than you found possible when you were a first-line supervisor.

It also helps to discuss certain aspects of your organizational activities with your superior and with some of your peers. Because they are impartial observers, they may see things not apparent to you in your managerial style and your approach to your subordinates. If you are willing to hear them out without prejudice, you can gain valuable insights.

Another means of clarifying and equalizing interpersonal relationships is your staff meetings. If you are observant, these meetings offer one of the better opportunities to compare your subordinates in many facets of their work, personalities, and potential. It is misleading to depend entirely upon performance record to make judgments of people, since you can never perfectly equate work loads and responsibilities. Neither can you equate the abilities of your various people. In group judgments, you will often find it necessary to weight some factors to make up for individual differences. This does not mean that you should try to make an amorphous, faceless mass out of your subordinates, but merely that such weighting is the only viable way to approach the matter objectively.

The clue to your personal operation in this area must be intense concentration. The slightest wandering from the course will encourage the obtrusion of factors which will distort your judgment. At this point, you will begin to realize in a very personal way the value of all the self-discipline you have been practicing since you first decided you wanted to be a manager. The objective approach to human problems must become habitual in your work. Your goal is to make it impossible for any of your subordinates ever to question the fairness of your actions with them. They do not have to agree with every decision you make, but their thinking must not be clouded by suspicions of your integrity if you intend to maintain a working team.

* * *

This chapter has considered your relationship with your subordinates. Conflicts will arise among your people, since they are both human and ambitious. You must know what methods to use to resolve these conflicts before they become catastrophic. You will also have to recognize and treat their jealousies of you and of each other. Because it is both logically appealing and functional, Management by Objectives is rapidly gaining ground throughout American business and industry. If you wish to remain competitive in the field, you should be prepared to know how to operate under this system. This chapter also dealt with the most common motivators for managers, and how you can put these motivators to work among your people. Finally, the necessity for cultivating the highest degree of objectivity possible in all your working relationships was discussed.

4

What Is the Occupational Disease of the Middle Manager?

MIDDLE managers as a group suffer from a common malady. They get restive and perturbed whenever they perceive a threat to the status quo. This reaction is understandable. The middle manager is the one largely responsible for the structuring of things as they now are. He contributed his significant pieces to the superstructure which has been supporting the enterprise for many years. He and his peers are comfortable with this product of their common effort; they know it has been functional; they are difficult to persuade that new days take new ways. For these reasons, middle managers often dare to defy directly policy directives sent down to them from executive offices. They do it by the easiest and most unbeatable of methods—they simply fail to implement the policy with supportive procedures, and the new method never gets off the ground.

At this point, before you have become a member of the middle group, you are doubtless thinking that it could never happen to you. You would be too much aware of the final penalty if you were actually discovered to be subverting executive action. However, when an entire group of middle managers conspires, either tacitly or overtly, to scuttle an executive decision, it is almost impossible to fix individual guilt, and executives have been known to retreat from this situation rather than challenge it. The smart boss is the one who knows when he is licked. It is possible that you may find yourself in this kind of situation once you are in middle management. Attempting to predict your behavior then on the basis of your position now is a risky undertaking. However, there are some factors which should influence your decisions in that setting.

First, attempting to maintain a solid and unyielding status quo in the face of external changing conditions will certainly hasten your anachronistic decay. You may protect your position temporarily, and you may apparently win the day, but when the time comes that you are actually out of step with the rest of the industry, or business at large, you had better be able to retire to coupon clipping and country-club golf. You will have had it in the business world. The graveyard is full of middle managers and executives who refused to recognize the passing of an old order and the birth of a new era. Time will not be beaten.

Second, although your executive echelon may beat a

temporary retreat from a united front of middle managers, they are, after all, the bosses, and they are not going to tolerate continued insubordination. Moreover, they record atypical behavior in a minutely documented little black book, and an accumulation of such actions has left more than one middle manager to wither on the vine and wonder why he never became an executive.

Third, the spinning of the web of isolation about you begins the moment you enter middle management. Job pressures and changed working habits will subtly rob you of the channels of communication you enjoyed as a first- or second-line supervisor. Your unsupported judgment may not—probably will not—be good enough to trust under conditions of change. You must have corroborative evidence from outside (neutral) sources before you cast your ballot for or against major change in your management area. Talking to your peers about these matters does not serve the purpose at hand; they have the same misperceptions of the real world under which you are suffering. You are going to have to send up flares both below you and completely outside your own organizational structure before you can be sure.

The fourth factor is the reactions of your subordinates. The common saying that you can often fool your boss, but never your subordinates has been proved true many times. They will always watch you closely. What you do then will in a large measure determine their definitive opinion of your judgment and your leadership. Since their ego involvement in changing the status quo is not as great as yours, they can be more objective about it—and they will be. The moment their consensus is that you have goofed a major decision, you have lost your effectivenesss as their leader. You may coast on for years under the impetus of controls and existing policy, but your chances to inspire them and lead them to new heights of achievement will have been largely vitiated.

There is an obvious key to this problem: Never allow yourself to make judgments about change on an emotional basis. If ever you will be called upon to exercise your full powers of discrimination and cold logic, it is now. If you give way to sentimentality, remember that one or more of your peers will not, and you will have unnecessarily handicapped yourself in the race for the next promotion. One saving grace keeps this sort of dilemma from being totally overwhelming. Almost never are you required to make impromptu or immediate decisions about major changes. They do not come about that way. Executive action itself is notoriously slow; they will give you all the lead time you need to make considered decisions concerning the way to go.

As we said, this is the besetting sin—the disease—common among middle management: a fierce defense of the status quo against all logic and against all tides. You can immunize yourself against this malady by using common sense, by properly mining the information readily available to you, and by employing a little concentrated thought.

Can You Fight City Hall?

In modern society, Don Quixote is a buffoon. Tilting at windmills is considered the ultimate in futility of effort and motivation. Yet, there are times when both the candidate and the member of middle management will have to take on the entire world to defend a principle and to salvage their self-respect. A multitude of forces converge on the middle echelons of management. Some are purely organizationally directed; others are entirely self-serving for the individuals exerting them. Unfortunately, at long intervals, a factor which bears the full weight of the approval of the executive level of management will become totally antithetical to all you hold proper and right. At these infrequent times, you have only one recourse—to take on the assembled might of the organization and fight it to a standstill. You will seldom win one of these encounters, but you will indicate your disapproval to all concerned.

There is a technique for assuming this attitude on those infrequent occasions when you find it necessary. First, and without fail, take your immediate superior into your confidence. *Never* surprise the boss. He may not agree with your position, and will probably attempt to dissuade you from it, but you will have reinforced his respect for you by having declared your intent. Second, pursue the same tactics as far up the line as you can get the attention of the managers involved. As you get closer to the origin of the policy you disclaim, you will find your reception increasingly colder and more impersonal. This is not germane; you are putting on record your disagreement with a proposed course of action. Unless you deviate too frequently, the same increment of respect will be gained at each level of your protest. The man who is ready to battle for his belief will not be denigrated, even by his opponents. The fact that you have registered your disapproval is bound to stimulate some rethinking at every level of contact. As we said, on rare occasions the lightning will strike, and you will win. In this circumstance, you will have gained significant clout.

One word of caution: It would be cowardly to trap your subordinates into backing what will in most cases be a losing cause. You should make it perfectly clear to all that this is *your* war, and that the members of your staff are not involved. Should their personal loyalty (or convictions) bring them to espouse your cause voluntarily, they are on their own.

We should consider the kinds of executive action which will elicit your disapproval. Obviously, in most cases they will concern problems with people rather than problems with things. Dispassionate decisions on the latter are easy to make; it is when the ten thousand independent variables associated with people get into the mix that doubts and problems arise. The kinds of problems with people which will raise a flare in your consciousness will most often be associated with a change in basic company philosophy. You will have accustomed yourself to a set pattern of company action; it is the deviant action which will arouse your animosity, and turn you against it.

Suppose, for example, that your enterprise has for many years been slightly paternalistic. Now, suddenly, it proposes an action which you think will repress personal autonomy and tend toward regimentation. This is the red flag which arouses your bullish reactions. You react, rather than act. We should face the fact that you are emotionally involved in this matter, and that your thinking is not as logical as your accustomed actions. Perhaps this may be all to the good. Even the best organization man in the world has his human and individualistic moments.

We have already said that you should clear your subordinates from any guilt by association. However, you still have an overpowering need to keep them completely aware of your thinking and of your progress toward your personal Golgotha. There is always the possibility that you may at any moment decide to retire from the fray to lick your wounds and recuperate. Nothing could be more catastrophic to your people than to leave them hanging, thinking you are still continuing your fight. Incidentally, no situation has more potential for increased personal commitment than this one. All of us are constantly searching subconsciously for a hero to worship. If we see our boss as the victim of "them," we instinctively elevate him to the position of martyr, and will be much more amenable to his leadership in other areas than we were before.

Let us now reset our perspective in this matter. You, as a prospective or actual middle manager, will undertake a defiant action only in the most rare and provocative of situations. A distinct challenge to your basic principles must be involved—one only a short distance this side of pulling the pin. Your emotions will be involved, and rationality will be a weapon rather than a basic fact or determinant of your plan of action. This is a rare exercise in individualism and personal determinism which you can afford only very infrequently. Your personal future is directly involved, as well as those of your subordinates and of your whole organization.

Although we have been discussing the pure opposite of the occupational disease of the middle manager, the practice of management deals with the juxtaposition of polarized elements, and with the harmonizing of polarized thinking. All we have said here is that, once in a while, it is urgently necessary for you to deviate from the standard.

WHAT IS OCCUPATIONAL DISEASE OF MIDDLE MANAGER?

How Are You at Compromise?

Because of his position in the hierarchy, and the gross pressures exerted on him from all directions, the middle manager must become adept at compromise if he is to survive. He simply cannot confront every challenge thrown at him and enter a fight to the finish over every problem. Quite quickly, he would be the one who was finished.

The art of compromise lies in developing skill in negotiation sufficient to ensure survival, and at the same time to preserve face for both parties. The key to the process is to be able to estimate quickly and closely how far you can retreat from your original position without incurring severe damage. The competent middle manager becomes so experienced that he can make this estimate in a matter of seconds for normal problem situations.

Another useful gambit is innate in the middle manager's position; that is, to deliberately put a packing fraction of overestimation into his original demand, so that he knows he will not be too badly hurt after negotiation. When your adversary also uses this maneuver, the opening position of the two is ridiculous, and everyone knows it. For example, if a middle manager knows he can perform his function without too much effort with a work force of 200 people, he might be tempted to staff up gradually to 240 people so that during the next reduction in force he could take a 20 percent cut without being paralyzed. Wasteful and perhaps dishonest as this practice may seem, it is used throughout business and industry. The ritual can become quite intricate when higher management recognizes what is going on, and proposes a cut of 35 percent. The middle manager breaks into a cold sweat when this is announced, and realizes that he will have to present an excellent rationale to his superiors to preserve his original target of 200 people.

It is a truism that no system has ever been invented for which a method of beating it was not forthcoming in a matter of hours. Obviously, the middle manager gets involved in a continuing game of wits in the areas of manpower and budgeting. The latter is an especially fertile field for exercising the middle manager's creative powers of negotiation and compromise. If he is more than half literate in the field of finance, he can employ dozens of tricks in budget design. The smart manager will accumulate and store his wealth in many little pockets, rather than risk his entire organization in a few large budget items. Then, if he gets hit with a blanket order of an overall 20 percent reduction in budget, he has some maneuvering ground in which to work, as well as good cover for his fiscal sleight of hand. Some of the small pockets can be wiped out entirely to achieve the necessary 20 percent without posing too much danger to the whole operation.

We must not forget that by far the greater number (and greater importance) of the manager's compromises will be in the area of interpersonal relationships. The most common type is the conflicts which arise among his subordinates. Some of these come from a genuine disagreement over the solutions to problems. Most functional compromises must be engineered by the superior if working relationships are not to be warped too far out of shape to be workable. Other conflicts are founded in power politics or jealousies among your people; here, compromise is even more essential to retain a reasonable working relationship. No one must be allowed to look too bad; no one must be

WHAT IS OCCUPATIONAL DISEASE OF MIDDLE MANAGER?

too consistently a winner in these clashes, or the department will be cut apart and become dysfunctional.

The middle manager must learn to keep himself strictly uninvolved in the personalities concerned. He will be personally down the tube if he identifies with either of the combatants; strict neutrality must be his forte.

So far, we have concentrated on conflicts within the middle manager's own organization. However, he will be forced to practice his art above, below, and to the side, to counterbalance other pressures constantly being imposed upon him. Engineering a successful compromise with the people working for you takes some doing, but the middle manager demonstrates real expertise when he succeeds in forcing a compromise with his own boss. This takes much more delicate maneuvering, and sounder strategy. Remember, your boss has been through the middle management mill, and knows all the ruses employed by managers in those ranks. You will have to be especially logical and brilliantly precise in setting up your pitches and presentations, if you want to impress your superior and get him going your way.

Ultimately, your middle management skill at compromise will meet its most severe test in your relationships with your peers. They usually have an axe to grind whenever they approach you. Each is at least as healthily self-centered as you, and each will have a certain amount of shrewdness and negotiating ability of his own. Moreover, since he is a peer, you are concerned about your batting average over the entire season. Hitting three for four in one game does not make you a batting champ. You will be extended to the limits of your ability and stamina in each encounter, and most certainly compromise in this area becomes a way of life rather than just a weapon. It's a crazy way to live, but an exciting one. The best device for self-protection is to think of it as a game, and to keep the anxiety level a few degrees below the boiling point. Remember, all can live, and none should have too many scars.

Are Your Interests Vested?

By the time you reach middle management, you will have a sizable chunk of your working life invested in your company. We all tend to value things according to their costs in time, money, or energy expended. So it is that middle managers come to feel that they have a vested interest in their organization in general. This is another major reason why middle managers so often strenuously resist significant changes in the structure of their operations. This feeling should, in general, be encouraged, since it is the ultimate in involvement and commitment by the manager. Our worry here is that such a strong feeling overshadows the balance so necessary in the thinking of the middle manager. He cannot afford to suffer from tunnel vision. Too much of the entire company is under his control for him to be narrow in his thinking. To reinforce: You should have a feeling of vested interest in the organization at large, but you should also know measures of protecting yourself against too strong a tie.

Do You Study Your Group?

Among the best of these methods is to have an organizational study made of your group at irregular intervals. The person, or team, who does the study must have unquestionable expertise in this complex procedure, and must be totally objective in his approach. This does not mean that you cannot have a company employee (or a group of them) perform this consultative service for you. One of your primary concerns in having the study made is to get a reading on the managers in your group—especially yourself. Your cooperation with the study team must be complete and wholehearted. No reticences are allowable for this trip under the glass. Any records called for must be surrendered. All questions must be answered fully and with complete candor. The report of the study team must be accepted and used with the same objectivity with which it was made.

Of course, one of the primary goals of the study will be to determine the extent of your vested interest quotient. If the study team has performed conscientiously and well, the results can give you a close estimate of this quotient for both yourself and your subordinates. The study team can also determine how that quotient is affecting the performance of your group.

A surprising number of organizational studies are undertaken for the wrong reason. For example, a manager may become worried about the fact that his turnover rate is too high, and may order a study of this one problem, forgetting that turnover rate is a symptom rather than a disease. If voluntary resignations are too frequent, there is a reason or reasons. These should be your objectives, if you wish to reduce the statistic to manageable proportions. A huge majority of cases of high turnover are associated with the managerial styles of the boss or bosses. Employees have become too sophisticated to tolerate managerial attitudes entirely out of consonance with their own.

Another good way of preventing, or controlling, excessive tunnel vision is to become active in your functional or professional organization. This activity is inherently broadening, and will force a widening of your perspective. Also, your participation will expose you to a constant stream of new activities and techniques, some of which are bound to be applicable to your group. In the first year of activity, you may find three or four methods which you will be able to adopt or adapt for your own use.

Also up for consideration is the protection of your subordinates from the same trouble you are guarding against in yourself. Fortunately, tunnel vision is not one of the socially unacceptable ills. You can talk to your subordinates about it without embarrassment to either party. Of course, the whole thing amounts to a state of mind—a point of reference—more than anything else. Your communication can be complete and unfettered, but your highest quality of leadership will be called upon to guide your people past this fascinating booby trap. It is entirely natural for a manager to become deeply engrossed in his organization and his company. On the one hand, we are constantly encouraging you to do just this; on the other, we are warning against too much attention to what we have said was a desirable activity. The rationale is the same as for many other situations: Don't overdo any good thing to the point of making a vice of it.

Possibly, under certain executive philosophies, this exercise on your part would be frowned upon. This is especially true in highly centralized or more conservative organizations, in which one of the primary objectives is the maintenance of the status quo under any circumstances, and against all odds. You could be completely excused for a certain amount of dissembling in this case. What you are doing is for your good and the eventual good of the organization. By now, you have reached middle management; the supererogation of your personal judgment becomes a necessity for successful operation. There are issues about which you are in a better position than anyone else to make decisions, including your boss and his. Naturally, you will not want to make a public issue of these occasions, but your duty to yourself and your people is clear. Seen in this light, you must proceed as your conscience and your intelligence dictate.

How Good Is Your Reaction Time?

Since the middle manager finds himself preoccupied with maintaining the status quo, he must also be concerned with how quickly he can react to intimations of impending change. That is, he must anticipate change quickly enough to have a reasonable chance of heading it off and preventing its implementation. Usually, he will be on his own in this matter.

You would be correct in assuming that this is an intuitive process. Time after time, middle managers become aware of the feeling of change before visible signs of it appear. Of course, if change is actually being planned, someone up there is aware of it. The middle manager becomes adept at interpreting nonverbal cues as they are generated in his areas of contact. He also has much practice in association of items which singly have not much import, but which in the aggregate are extremely meaningful. Mostly, he must be able to attach these cues to their originators, and trace the path to the prime mover behind the proposed change. He must identify his adversary.

It is obvious how important is the matter of reaction time in this process. The manager's only possible chance of forestalling implementation of the new policy or procedure is to project himself into the action arena before too deep a commitment has been made at the executive level. His superiors will be much more amenable to his arguments if they have not gone visibly a great distance toward solidification of the proposal.

Change may be instituted from below as well as from above. When you become a middle manager, you must develop an acuteness of perception about your subordinates' reactions as great as the perception you maintain about your superiors. The Young Turks you are managing will be full of ideas and proposals. Your interests will be best served if you are aware of them early, and have time to make value judgments of proposals, well in advance of any commitment. This will entail more than normal monitoring of the usual channels of communications. Everything said before about intuitive response should be reinforced for this situation. The chances are great that a subordinate will be reluctant to talk much about an idea until he has it well conceptualized. He knows the value of a good presentation as well as you do. There are unmistakable signs, however, of the gestation of an idea. One or more of your subordinate's people will undoubtedly be involved in the action, and they will be more likely to give hints than will the man most directly concerned.

Perhaps at this point we should interject a warning. All we are talking about here is the middle manager's natural tendency to be concerned about the general prospect of impending change. It is not that he is categorically opposed to change per se, but that his own protection demands that he know the nature of any change well in advance of its institution. He is the core around which the factors generated by any change will operate. He has become used to being the man in the middle, but will demand a partial say about the numbers and kinds of changes.

The other possibility for the imposition of new activities comes from the manager's peer groups. Changes in other functional areas can be expected to have concomitant effects on his operation. Here, reaction time is probably of the greatest importance to your operation as a middle manager. Since you have no direct control over the actions of your opposite numbers, you will need a much better planned and executed campaign to defeat an undesirable change. This is especially true if the peer proposing a new procedure which will affect you does not report to your superior. The farther up the managerial hierarchy you have to work to get a controlling decision, the harder your job will be in heading off the change.

One major force is working for you: You can train yourself to become generally aware and alert. By working hard at it, you can form a habit of responding to subtle cues, and be in small danger of being surprised. The average person responds to surprise with panic, which becomes a great disadvantage in his battle to head off the new proposal. We have made an assumption throughout this discussion that your judgments of the proposals will be good. If this is not true, no amount of alertness and no speed of reaction time will be of service to you. From the standpoint of protection of your working group, the necessity of developing teamwork and cooperation among your subordinates is clear as crystal. You simply cannot do the entire job by yourself; there are too many places to be, and too many cues to read simultaneously, for any one man.

The other corollary of the situation is the necessity of operating from a clearly defined and carefully enforced managerial philosophy. The course through middle management, and possible advancement to the executive level, cannot be left to chance. Only when you have a master chart to go by will your navigation be functional. If you ever discover that your philosophy is more than slightly out of synchronization with that of the enterprise, you have only two ways to go. You can either revamp your own thinking, or you can sever your connection with the business. At the middle and higher echelons, a true deviant has small chance of survival. The possibility of changing the thinking and actions of all the other members of management is microscopic. This fact is the cause for no little part of the mobility of good managers from one organization to another.

Now—What Is Your Pressure Coefficient?

Ever since you first began thinking about entering supervision, people have been telling you about the pressures of management jobs. You found out for yourself when you became a supervisor that they were correct. Now we must inform you that these pressures will be multiplied several times when you become a middle manager. Your responsibility will be greater; your peers will be more experienced; your subordinates will be pushing you; your superiors will lean heavily upon you. Pressure will be generated in large amounts simply from the grossly increased number of details which will cross your desk. We say details, but each of these items will have more importance to the enterprise than any single decision you made at the first line. Moreover, you will have less time to spend on any of these items than you would like before being called upon to make a decision.

Establishing the fact that there will be increased pressures in a middle management job is not nearly so important as being able to forecast your reaction to them. Some people respond well to pressure, and do their best work when under its impetus. They think more clearly, make better decisions, and meet deadlines more easily when they are forced to do so. At the opposite pole are those who freeze when pressured, and are unable to work efficiently. They either spin their wheels in furious but useless activity, or do nothing at all and simply wait the coming of the executioner. There are many degrees of reaction between these two extremes. Before you finally cast your decisive vote for a life in middle management, you must make a personal assessment of how pressure affects you. We are all aware of how continued pressure can give rise to unpleasant—even dangerous—physical reactions. Ulcers, high blood pressure, heart attacks, and many other ailments can sometimes be traced to pressures in our daily living. Other even more insidious psychosomatic ailments may come from the same source.

Few of us would willingly accept this kind of burden for any kind of job. There are managers by the dozen beautifully prepared to take on heavier responsibility except for an inability to live with increased pressures. You should not depend entirely upon your own analysis of this situation. Discuss it with friends, and above all, with your family physician. These people can help you come to a decision on this matter, but they cannot make it for you. You will have to give the final word.

Increased pressures on the job can also have devastating effects on your interpersonal relationships. Friendships of long standing have been shattered by tensions on the job. Aside from the personalities involved, if you react unfavorably to pressure, your subordinates will probably fall off in productivity and show reduced quality of the work done. They are as human as you; if the boss is harried and tense, they will ordinarily respond in like manner. The whole climate of your work area can be darkened and made sinister by your mannerisms. One of the main casualties will be the confidence of your people, and eventually of your superiors as well. We turn for leadership to those who remain calm and serene in the midst of the battle.

It is urgent that you remember the tremendous power of cultivated self-control. By concentrating on this characteristic, it is quite possible that you can learn to live with pressures you would have thought unbearable before. This is a good reason for maintaining a regular quiet time as a part of each working day. You always have enough discretionary time to devote a little of it to peaceful contemplation of your situation, and for some personal planning. When we plan properly for pressures, they lose a large part of their potency. Another thing we tend to forget is that our subordinates not only can, but will want to, share some of your pressures with you. They will acknowledge this as meaning that you recognize their worth to your organization, and they will perform at a higher rate than you had thought possible.

* * *

This chapter looked at middle management's traditional and universal unwillingness to take on major change. The middle manager has fought long and hard to attain his present position, which is anchored securely to the old way of operation. Any real innovation presents a threat to his security, or so it appears to him. Thus, middle management often becomes the burial ground of new ideas germinated either above or below the middle echelon of management. The middle manager becomes adept at fighting city hall, since he is bound to maintain his own position at any cost. One of his best methods of doing this is compromise, through which he may lose a few battles, but never the war.

The middle manager thinks of himself as having a vested interest in the organization, since he has invested a large chunk of his adult life in attaining his present position. To be successful, he must have very good reaction speed; his best chance is to beat his opponent to the punch. Above all, he must be able to live with unremitting pressure coming at him from all directions.

How Are You at Politics?

WE have already seen that the middle manager will at times behave as if he were a student of *The Prince*. For some managers, this conduct would seem to be a must; others find it unnecessary and distasteful. The matter of manipulation of employees comes up time and again in any extended look at the field of management. So much opprobrium has become attached to the term "manipulation" that we tend to forget there is a positive side to manipulation, and that this is the real reason for the job of the manager.

Nevertheless, in deference to the widely held belief about manipulation, we shall take this look at it on the assumption that an honest manager will feel uncomfortable if he is accused of Machiavellianism. He feels degraded, and immediately becomes defensive. Implicit in this concept is the understanding that the employee is being maneuvered to the advantage of the boss, or the enterprise, without his knowledge. A majority of managers state candidly that they would have no hesitation about performing such actions with their people if they had their agreement in advance. This is to say that the harm is in the lack of communication, rather than in the net result to the individual. The ethics of this position are indeed debatable. It says, in effect, that it is all right to commit mayhem if we tell our victims about it beforehand.

How Do You React to Machiavellianism?

We would be far less than realistic to presume to tell you, a mature and seasoned member of management, what your personal code of ethics should be. You have long since crystallized it, and have been operating under it for years. We are concerned, on the other hand, with the effect your standards of conduct will have on your career as a manager —and so are you.

We would also be out of tune with the times if we did not acknowledge that numerous old mores are currently under severe fire, and in danger of being replaced by more liberal views. The most potent of the independent variables on the current scene is the change in relationship between subordinate and superior over the past two decades. In fact, the use of the terms "superior" and "subordinate" is in danger of making this book itself anachronistic.

So You Want to Be a Manager!

The executive management of many flourishing businesses are following a course deliberately designed to blur the former definition of these titles. Whenever possible, they prefer not to use them at all, and will tend to substitute "colleague" or "associate." If this change is the result of sincere belief, and is an implementation of true company philosophy, the use of the methods of Machiavelli are automatically precluded. If we are truly intent on making the job of the manager more like that of an administrator, and want to zero in on the contribution of each employee to the total enterprise, we can no longer operate with anything less than complete candor toward our people.

One fact far from universally understood is that this decision can be made at any level in the company organization for the part of the enterprise responsible to a given manager. If authority has been delegated, it is perfectly possible for a Theory Y manager (who believes, according to Professor McGregor, that people are good and want to work) to run his group under this posture while reporting to a dyed-in-the-wool Theory X manager (who believes that people hate to work and need constant supervision). So long as the Theory Y manager maintains his accountability, his methodology can be his own. This pragmatic application of the theory of decentralization is increasing throughout industry. Some cynics mutter about the end justifying the means, but in truth this is a pure and simple application of a practical approach to modern management. Since a rising swell of independence is definitely occurring in the attitude of nonmanagement personnel, this is probably the most viable attitude you as a manager can adopt. There are some conditions with which we have to make our peace if we want to go on. The cream of the jest is that once made, this decision can immensely simplify your working life.

As we said, this stance would make it both practically and theoretically impossible for you as a manager to subscribe to a manipulative sort of management. The two positions simply are not congruent. One automatic result of this situation will be clearer and sharper communications everywhere in the functioning organization. This end will not have to be pursued with blood, sweat, and tears, since it is a perfectly predictable outcome of your operating policy. Naturally, the atmosphere will be much more conducive to creativity and innovation. In fact, your job as a manager will now be to exercise the rein a little more often than you have before.

The above is in one sense parallel to the subject of this chapter. You are not really so much concerned with Machiavellianism in the line as you are with how it will affect you in your peer relationships. More than one manager keeps a strict double standard in his business actions. He is a model of probity in dealing with his peers, and at the same time an untrustworthy assassin when prowling among his competitors. This is not an unusual mental outlook. We treat our own with honor and respect; in the jungle, we use predatory methods. Once again, we are not here to argue the morality of this, but to be sure that you are forewarned and prepared for the eventuality. Many hoodlums are also models of domestic virtue. Your obligation is to protect yourself from their depradations while on the job. Here is another frame of reference which calls for clear thinking and some final decisions. The way you go will determine your success as a middle manager, and will govern your advancement into the executive echelons.

So You Want to Be a Manager!

Are You an Opportunist?

The word "opportunist" is one of many in the English language which is frustrating because it sounds as if it should have a good connotation, but does not. Of course, the twist in opportunism is its implication of lying in wait for opportunities to turn to one's personal advantage. Therefore, the noun is reserved for a medium grade of intended insult. Yet we would be less than realistic to deny that middle managers have survived for extended periods of time, and have even prospered, through no other long-range planning than to seize an opportunity and distort it to their use.

Probing this situation leads to some interesting observations. For example, real intelligence is required to recognize an opportunity in time to take advantage of it. Decisions must be made quickly and fearlessly. Action to implement the decisions must be precise and crisp. We are saying, then, that the managers described above exhibit many of the characteristics we want in management personnel. The fatal flaw lies in the lack of personal integrity they show, and in their failure to put the good of the enterprise at the top of their priorities.

We shall make the natural assumption that this is not your method of working, and that you will continue to operate with a decent code of business ethics. The biggest remaining question then becomes: How do you protect yourself from these vandals when their campaign impinges on yours? We could beg the question by saying that we will fight fire with fire, and will meet this adversary on his own grounds. To do so would of course vitiate any pretense of ethical operations.

HOW ARE YOU AT POLITICS?

There are two phases to this kind of contest. The first is to establish beyond the faintest doubt the motivation of the manager in question. This is a dangerous gambit, because in some cases by the time you have verified his opportunism, it is too late to do anything about it. The only answer is to be consistently vigilant, and go into action at the earliest possible moment.

This brings us to phase two of the contest, which consists of a thoroughgoing ventilation of the entire episode. The one thing your adversary cannot stand is to have his position exposed to his superiors, his peers, or his subordinates in this posture. Once these people are convinced of his venality, he will be totally deprived of allies. Moreover, he will be in grave danger of actually losing his job, since his managers will be most apt to translate the word "opportunism" into "treachery."

If you have qualms about your part in this series of events, forget them. This action comes clearly and undeniably within the sphere of your managerial responsibility. You have a further duty here which may be unpleasant to you—to use this incident as a learning opportunity for those who report to you. One occurrence of this sort may just make Christians out of any waverers among your people.

What Are Your Operating Rules?

This is not the first time we have mentioned your code of business ethics. It might not be amiss to make a slight detour to flesh out this rather abstract concept. Essentially, we are speaking of conceptualization and verbalization of a hopefully short, but inclusive, set of operating rules. The key word is decency. We need to establish bench marks against which to measure our plans and projected actions. This is not as clear cut and definitive as it might seem. One of the penalties of our increasingly complex social structure is the rapid disappearance of blacks and whites, with a concomitant proliferation of grays. It is no longer a simple matter to judge the moral value of an intended course of conduct. Too many variables intervene and cloud the basic issue.

Is price fixing inherently immoral, or is it a pragmatic method of self-protection in the industrial jungle? What is our ethical involvement when we recommend early retirement for a twenty-year man who is still performing competently on his present assignment, but who has obviously peaked out and is blocking upward mobility in his line? The many shades of gray make us wonder whether we have suddenly become color blind.

One fact has been established: No enlightened modern manager can deny that his involvement in his enterprise carries social responsibilities which are larger than the job itself. We no longer can make decisions in these areas purely on the business facts available. We are responsible for the impact of our decision on the work group, the enterprise, the community, and the nation. This staggering responsibility is more than some middle managers find possible to live with.

Of course, the formulation of your personal code of ethics has taken a lifetime. We would be naive to think that you will drastically change your thinking about these things when you are at the point of entering middle management. The most we can hope for is an occasional reevaluation and reaffirmation of mores already solidly set in your daily living. However, since the frontal, direct attacks on your tenets will occur continuously, you do need frequent reinforcement of their essential validity. The final test will be your extended ability to live comfortably with yourself, subjected to no major doubts about your course of action.

Incidentally, a serendipitous corollary to this process will be your renewed vigor in your work, and your increased confidence in expected results. This lowering of your anxiety level will be reflected in your overall attainments. Even your relationships with your working companions will be noticeably better. So, all your effort will have been worthwhile, and will truly show the profit which was the intent of the opportunist.

Can You Commit Yourself?

The novice politician encounters most of his trouble, and makes most of his mistakes, by agonizing too long about committing himself. He forgets that before he can be considered for office—either political office or a new job in the company—the rest of the populace must know where he stands and what principles he espouses. Ever since you became a supervisor you have been aware that politics has a place in industrial life. Now, as you prepare to enter middle management, it must be apparent to you that the political tempo and sharpness have increased noticeably at this new level. The stakes are higher; the competition is keener; the rivals are stronger and more deeply involved.

You certainly should not assume from the above that you must hurry in picking your team and declaring your commitment. Rushing is just as fatal to your chances as is hesitation after the picture is clearly drawn. You must force yourself to take the time necessary to assess the situation, and to determine with what group you want affiliation. There will be groups. They coalesce around the stronger leaders at each level of the hierarchy, and all concerned know who the members are in each group.

At this point you will have to make one of your more delicate decisions. You may decide that your immediate superior is not the one for whom you want to declare. Many factors are involved in this choice: his strength as a leader, his political savvy, the power and placement of his friends and supporters, and most important of all, his fundamental principles and beliefs. If the summation of these leads you to decide there is a stronger candidate, you would be doing yourself no favor to join his camp and commit yourself to a losing cause. At this point comes the delicacy of the choice mentioned above. *You still owe him basic organizational loyalty and support, and this will not change.*

We should reinforce this point: You must make a careful study of your new environment before you decide whose camp to enter. This means a quick and positive effort at getting to know many new people at this echelon. You have to be able to evaluate their strengths, their weaknesses, their methods of operation, and the basic characteristics of their organizations. More than anything else, you must know with whose operational principles you can live, and with whose you cannot. The commitment you are about to make at this point will determine your entire future in the enterprise, barring accidents such as a sudden and unexpected merger at the top, with new executives moved in at that level.

It is imperative that you use several sources of intelligence in assembling your data. Certainly, your own observations must be high on the usage list. Trusted employees on your own staff can give you valuable information from their contacts. Key people outside the company, such as long-time vendors, are invaluable in some cases for their special knowledge of individuals. Sheer chance can have its impact, such as information picked up from strangers in outside organizations to which you belong. None of these should be discounted until you have had a chance to weigh and evaluate the facts you have gleaned.

The strategy you are employing—the game you are in—are not dishonorable in any sense of the word. An open entry into company politics is no more disgraceful than an entry into the political arena in your community or state. In fact, everyone will expect you to make this move by the time you are in middle management. The only person there who can remain uncommitted is the man who has decided that he has gone as far as he wants to go. Even he may be forced at times to indicate which camp he identifies with, in the event of power struggles. If you are strategically placed, it is impossible to declare and maintain neutrality.

The matter of your eventual political commitment is of great importance to you because it is by nature nearly as final and irrevocable as was your original decision to opt for the company and make a run for supervision. Once made, your choice will become public property almost immediately. People being what they are, the fact that you have made a choice will generate a certain number of natural enemies. True commitment means emotional involvement, and two of the stronger emotions are love and hate. Conversely, your group of (at least political) friends is also instantly established, and you have indicated your resource personnel for in-company managerial action from here on out. This is your personal Rubicon.

At this point, we should examine your situation if your decision has put you in the camp opposite your immediate superior. This situation is unfortunate, and will complicate your managerial life as long as you continue to report to him. He would be only human if he were to reserve complete trust in your intentions and activities. There will always be something of "I wonder what he meant by that?" in his attitude toward you. Why not? How will you feel when one of your favorite subordinates does the same thing to you someday? It will mean that you must work harder to achieve the same results, and even when you achieve them, you can expect less than normal recognition or praise. The best you can ever hope for is an armed truce, and a lack of open hostility. Whatever the result, you have a clear and unceasing duty to maintain technical loyalty to your boss as long as you are with him. Anything less would lead to complete chaos and an untenable position for both of you.

To recapitulate: You *will* have to commit yourself in the political battle; you *will* have to keep your normal operating efficiency; and you *will* have to take your personal risks and rebuffs if you are to have any hope of further advancement.

Can You Pick a Winner?

In the preceding segment we skirted the edges of the topic before us now. It is one thing to pick sides in a general political alignment; it is entirely different to zero in on an individual and bet what amounts to the future of your career on his ability to rise to the top. Your winner, you might say, will have to be excellent in all the functions of management. He will be expected to know how to plan, organize, direct, and control; his performance in these areas must be as expert as his knowledge. His attention to production, costs, and quality must be close and unremitting. His relationships with his people must be on an even and workable keel, although actual friendship is not required. Communications from him and through him must be concise, sharp, and definitive. His attention to administrative details must be uninterrupted in a way that will annoy no one. Yes indeed, all these things he must do well on a continuing basis—but these are essentially the minimal job requirements of every successful middle manager. You will have to look further for the criteria by which you pick a winner and assure your own continued success. There is no universal agreement about the bench marks which forecast upward mobility, but a few are irrefutable.

The first is exceptional speed and accuracy in decision making. The winner must consistently beat his competitors to the draw and to the target. He may have the reputation for making his decisions on the basis of intuition, but if you pin him down, you will find him able to give an entirely reasonable (and closely reasoned) explanation of his proposed actions. The process is complete, and his only variance from his peers is in his ability to go through it with exceptional celerity and to come up with the right answer.

The second characteristic of the man with executive potential is unusual ability in innovation. Not only is he prolific in the production of new ideas, but he is not afraid to try them if they pass the tests of his judgment. In other words, a talent for innovation is associated with a great willingness to take risks. He is not afraid to depart from the normal route toward his goal if he thinks he sees a better path. At the same time, he will be able to calm the fears of his subordinates, and elicit their full cooperation and support in the new venture. The product of these individual and group factors will be an unusually high esprit de corps. An energizing excitement will pervade his organization.

The potential executive's proficiency to judge people will be far above average. In this area, he may admit rather wryly that he is sometimes guilty of making intuitive judgments, but for the most part he can back his decisions with data extremely pertinent and surgically sharp in their delineation of basic character. Another feature of his judgment of people is a total disregard of his personal feelings about them. It is irrelevant whether he likes, dislikes, or is completely indifferent to them as individuals. He is interested in results, and will pick those people he believes can produce them.

You should never put your money on the nose of one of the potential executives until you have satisfied yourself that he has great powers of conceptualization. His next move will be to the echelon where results are judged almost entirely on his ability to conceptualize. You need not necessarily be personally close to a manager in order to

HOW ARE YOU AT POLITICS?

judge this trait. It will stand out in his managerial record and actions, begging you to evaluate it. A little extra effort in this area is often rewarded by superiors with job enrichment even before a promotional vacancy occurs. The potential winner may be operating like an executive before he gets the actual position. This amounts to on-the-job training without the usual attendant risks. At the same time, his people are receiving high-caliber training for their entry into middle management. As a preparation for group advancement, this training is analogous to being able to attend a great university rather than a second-rate one.

Once your candidate for winner has been evaluated and selected, there remains the necessity of effecting a de facto alliance with him. It is not necesassary that you ever work for him. In fact, it may turn out that you will never be directly in his line. We are speaking of the informal organization, which at this level is always present and always a factor to be reckoned with in the management of the enterprise. Organizational consultants draw up their own functional charts when studying any business. What they want to know is who really runs the shop. Your act of joining forces with your projected winner will probably never be verbalized by you or openly acknowledged by him. Yet your mutual understanding will be excellent, and you will find it possible to work together smoothly and productively.

From a pragmatic viewpoint, this alliance will increase perceptibly your influence on what goes on in the organization. Moreover, your communications with the fountainhead will be more direct and meaningful. Obtaining information in your hands just a shade faster will work to your advantage in your competitive position. Remember, too, that this alliance does not have to be a one-shot occurrence. If your company is large, there will be several likely candidates with executive potential, and it could do no harm for you to have good working relationships with several of them. Of course, one obstacle to this is that the two or three strongest candidates will be on opposite sides of the political fence, and it may not be possible to enter into a complete détente with both sides. You would not want to do so under any circumstances.

How Strong Are Your Allies?

If you have made the considered decision to enter the political arena in your business, one more element must be thoroughly checked out before you openly declare your position. That is the number and strength of your allies—your gang. This group will be composed of your peers, and may or may not be graced by the presence of one of the winners we described earlier. Infrequently, a heavyweight from a level or two above you may also be included.

The group coalesces from a perceived common need to reinforce each other in gaining their personal goals. It is the equivalent of a mutual insurance company whose members pool their assets and agree to draw upon this common capital when a debt is incurred by one of them, or the company of volunteer fire fighters who come together at the sound of the alarm. It is not a working group, but a special task force.

Your probability of success in further advancement past middle management will be closely correlated to the

HOW ARE YOU AT POLITICS?

caliber of the people in this group. However, it is formed not entirely by your volition. Other factors enter in, and in many respects you might say its emergence is a matter of chance. First of all, there has to be a mutual recognition of advantages to be gained from political grouping, of something in it for each person concerned. Oddly enough, this basic reason for alliance does not always work out on a selfish plane. Many times, the group decides which of its members is the strongest possibility for a given opportunity, and then will unite behind him with a power that is almost unbeatable. The membership is willing to defer for one round the realization of personal ambitions in order to demonstrate the force of their combined efforts. If they are successful in their ploy, they know that the winner has incurred a heavy load of personal debt to each of his backers, so in the long run no one has lost anything, and the possibility remains for a handsome gain.

So, as we have indicated, it is urgently necessary that you accurately understand the strengths of the people in your political pack. You will need not only an overall summation, but positive and detailed knowledge of each one's strengths and weaknesses all along the line. Company politics are exactly like regular politics in that we can recognize those who are spellbinders with the crowd, those who are extremely effective with a small group, and those who shine in face-to-face confrontations. Additionally, no political group should be formed without the inclusion of one member who excels at strategy and timing.

It would be immature to think that such a group would be successful in every campaign it pursues. Remember, this is your first association with such an activity, and you will be taking on other older and more experienced groups which have been through the lists many times. Actually, it would be little short of miraculous if you were not to take two or three severe beatings before you came home with a winner. These first engagements will have to be charged off to experience, and if you do so, they can be even more valuable than an encounter you might win by a fluke. In these skirmishes your brothers will be tested, and you will learn with finality which of them can be counted on as steadfast and worthy allies. From this action will come permanent combinations of strength which will last you for the rest of your career.

You must not forget that you will also be subject to evaluation by all the other members of your coterie. They will be looking at your pluses and minuses just as you do at theirs, and for the same personal reasons. There is no better illustration of the two-way street than this kind of functional coalition. By the same token, your group will be judged, individually and collectively, by the rest of management on your performance in these battles. This informal, and officially unrecognized, activity is highly regarded by executive management as a proving ground for promotional material from middle management. The fact that at first you may not pull the rabbit from the hat will not be held against you if your general performance is deemed worthy by the occupants of mahogany row.

Considerable transfer of learning occurs from political experience outside the business scene. All of us have been vaguely aware of a young middle manager who developed a sudden interest in becoming president of his parent-teacher association or fraternal organization, or perhaps in gaining a seat on the city council. The fundamental precepts of political action are the same whatever the context, just as are the activities of management itself. You are the best judge of your available time and energy, and you might decide that it would be worthwhile to make a sortie of this kind. One beneficial result from winning one of these offices would be your company's official recognition of your sense of community responsibility. It redounds on the good reputation of the enterprise to have a manager in a position of recognized public trust.

A word of warning: The undeniable fascination of this activity could wheedle you away from a proper concentration on your own job. This would be extremely dangerous, and could seriously hamper your long-range objectives. Once more, we must remind you of the paramount importance of maintaining balance in your various duties. You must make frequent—nearly daily—value judgments about the apportionment of your energies and labor at this, the point of your entry into middle management.

How's Your Killer Instinct?

One of the critical elements of political activity is not pleasant to discuss. Early in your decision-making process about whether you truly want to be promoted into middle management, you will have to evaluate how ruthless you really are. In your political engagements there will probably come a time when you will have to cut your enemy down by sometimes ruthless means. This realization is disturbing to most men the first time they face it. The identity of the person standing in your way is totally irrelevant. He may be a stranger to you; he may be a friend of long standing. In either event, if you want to win, you will have to dispose of your adversary. The only shred of comfort left you in your humanitarian considerations is that, at this level, a man may survive one or two of these debacles and still go ahead later. One level higher, this is seldom true. Once out, there it is. About the only choice you have is of the method of elimination you will use. Perhaps one may be a little more humane than others.

The most common gambit is to lure your enemy into making an obvious error in business judgment. If you have considerable liaison with his group, this act will be easier to accomplish. The plot will be rather elaborate, but will hinge on an act of omission on your part. It is similar to the failure of a general to bring up reinforcements at exactly the right time. If you gallop up with full fanfare five minutes too late, all you can do then is commiserate with him over his misfortune. He knows what has happened but will never admit it, because he would look too much the fool not to have seen before what was brewing. On the surface, your relationship will appear unaltered.

The most insidious (and the most dangerous) method is that of character assassination, an extremely subtle and devious procedure. It is based on the fact that all of us are human, and will perform many acts which appear suspect if viewed in a certain light. It is your job in this tidy little game to be sure that the light is on him in exactly the proper wattage. The dangerous part of this tactic is that if you are discovered, it will be your character suffering from a fatal disease.

In these situations, your target will be a peer. One of the more direct, and apparently open, methods is to carry the attack on him to his superior. Here, you must gather much more valid data, and be prepared to substantiate each point of conflict with chapter and verse. Even then, you will have a heavy inertia to overcome the superior's obvious bias toward one of his trusted and valuable employees. Therefore, this technique should be employed only when you are clearly in the right. It is no place for iffy considerations. However, if you are successful, you will win the entire war, and your competition is dead.

Another obvious point of attack is through your rival's own organization. This tactic should be employed only if you have a reasonable assurance of some definite weak spots in his leadership activities. Your success will depend upon the demonstrable presence of disgruntled and dissatisfied subordinates, who can be wooed into active subversion. They must become your direct accomplices in what amounts to a palace revolution. If your henchmen are key figures, your rival may suddenly wake up to find his house termite ridden and no longer habitable. One point must be kept in mind here: You are leaving on the table some large IOUs which will inevitably have to be redeemed at face value plus interest somewhere down the line. The other memento of this occasion will be an implacable enemy in the form of the betrayed superior. He will never forgive your having destroyed his group.

We have been discussing things which are ordinarily not formalized or put in print, but the theme of this chapter is a pragmatic recognition of the facts of life in the modern business world. If we accept the premise of serious commitment to advancement, we have to recognize these fundamental verities. Now let's reverse the field, and point out the significant numbers of middle managers who have arrived at that station with minimal or no personal involvement in politics. These are the ones so loaded with natural ability that they find it unnecessary to engage in what they consider to be a demeaning game. If you are in that category, you are to be congratulated. Even so, you may find it impossible to make the last high hurdle into the executive atmosphere without using political tools. The positions become fewer and fewer; the contestants are stronger and stronger.

* * *

This chapter recognized a fact of business life: the presence and continued volatility of political action. Involved will be your personal mental outlook and your reaction to operating under the principles of Machiavelli. You must avoid falling into the trap of conducting yourself as an opportunist, since this is far too loose and dangerous a method of action. Now, as never before, you must be prepared to commit yourself to one side or the other of the political arena, but only after a complete and accurate analysis of the situation.

6

What Is the State of Your Development Plan?

IF you had anything to do with preparation for your promotion into supervision, you probably worked from some kind of development plan. This was a calculated effort to grow in those areas where you recognized weakness, and to make still greater capital of your inherent strengths. This may not have been the case, however, if you were picked by your superiors for promotion. In that event, you will still be ignorant about how self-development plans are created and administered.

We must also (sorrowfully) admit that many men forget the need for further development once they gain entry into the ranks of management. This can happen for two reasons:

Either the supervisor becomes and remains so busy that he convinces himself he has no time for self-development; or he makes the considered decision that this level is as far as he wants to go. Neither of these excuses is valid. A supervisor *always* has time to do the things he considers important. That is, consciously or otherwise, he decides which of his tasks take priority, and attends to the urgent ones. Self-development comes within this category if you have any desire for further advancement. You cannot depend on your natural growth on the job to prepare you for promotion or to call upper management's attention to you again, since all your peers are also growing and developing naturally on the job. You must devote specific attention and careful planning to the proposed extra activities to force your growth in areas of need. Even if you do decide that you want to go no further, progress is so rapid in these times that you will have to improve your performance merely to ensure staying where you are.

How Do You Prepare a Development Plan?

This book has attempted to counsel you on how to evaluate and prepare a plan for growth. The important thing is that you have such a plan, and that you develop and maintain a timetable for its accomplishment. If you have not been following one, there are two ways to approach the problem. The first, and easier, is to look at the old plan which was successful in pulling you into management. Several of its items might still be germane to your main problems. Perhaps with only a little upgrading, or updating, you could have the skeleton of a procedure which would work for you now.

If you have never before operated with a plan, now is certainly the time to enlist the aid of your superior and the management development specialist in designing one. It is always difficult to put into proper perspective our own weaknesses. We need help here, especially the first time around a developmental cycle. If properly conceived, your developmental goals will be time limited and self-liquidating. The optimal time increment is six months, since this length will keep your objectives constantly before you. That is not to say you might not have some objectives on a one-, two-, or even five-year time span, but the function itself is better geared to a six-month period than to any other.

By this time, you are well aware of the value of personal discipline. Certainly since you have been in supervision, this has been borne home to you many times a day. Now it will be necessary to maintain your unremitting efforts at development against the numberless snags and booby traps which will be thrown in your path. Once you have decided to begin this regimen, the interruptions constantly forced upon you will frequently make you feel frustrated. As we said, it is all a matter of the priority you put upon this activity as an aid to help you get your next promotion. One or several forcible rearrangements of your living schedule will occur while you are building this plan into your daily life. However, it must not be allowed to interfere with the day-to-day accomplishment of your present job.

Do You Have Allies?

It is heartening to report that you will find some willing allies to help you achieve this goal. Your line of management will certainly be delighted, since whether you are promoted or not, your performance on your present job cannot help but improve. There will be an upswing in the tone of your entire work group as your personal performance gets better.

It will not be enough that you design (with help) and install this plan into your working life. You must also assume the responsibility for a continuous, day-by-day monitoring of progress in all facets of your pattern for growth. This objective judgment is one of the most worthwhile goals you could establish in your program, since it will become increasingly important in your overall performance from here on out. The most productive control you could build into your system would be to set up specific standards for comparison along the time continuum of your plan. We are speaking of the milestones recognizable on the path to one of your major objectives. One or more failures to achieve these milestones will naturally alert you to make a thorough reevaluation of your entire program. It could be a sign of improper emphasis on one element of your development.

In any event, it is to be hoped that you are aware of the basic necessity for setting up a program and establishing the mechanics for administering it with the least possible disruption of your normal work life. When it is really workable, your plan for growth should be an aid rather than a hindrance for getting today's job done satisfactorily. The two should complement each other, rather than act in any way as mutually disturbing influences. When proper design and implementation have been utilized, the end product will be a more functional and smoothly running operation, now and in the future.

Are You Shoring Up, or Building?

We have not reinforced enough the necessity for some fine discrimination in the design and implementation of your development program. There is a vast difference between rebuilding a worn-out structure and putting up a new one. The announced objective of this process is the creation of a better you. Our emphasis is notably on the positive side; our interest is much less in repairing weaknesses than in creating strengths. The difference between these two concepts is 180 degrees. Psychologists tell us that the normal man's most creative period occurs in his late thirties and throughout his forties. If you remain alert, and are willing to expend the time and energy, you should be making some of your best contributions now and for the next decade. This is the time when you will forge your career and your reputation, for better or worse. The decisions you make now, and for the next few years, will affect the rest of your working life in the most important ways.

The most critical test to be put to you is your determination to go ahead. There will be many roadblocks in your path, both those which are natural and those which are designed and put there deliberately by your superior. He is concerned with the depth and steadfastness of your commitment to success. What makes this test situation more traumatic than others is that you are working so much in the intangible and unquantifiable areas, and that you are the object of the test. Your ego involvement in the entire process is so great that it is easy to lose perspective. You are now under the gun with an intensity you have never experienced before. No one else can accept responsibility for the final appraisal of your development program, or put the last touches on its design.

Once this perception is clear, the procedure is relatively simple. Every element of your development program must be put under the glass for intense scrutiny, and then subjected to what would amount to thorough physical and chemical testing with an inanimate object. Your criteria must be selected with utmost care, and if any aspect of the segment under examination shows the slightest flaw, it should be discarded immediately without compunction. The vehicle which is to get you from here to there must have no feature subject to the slightest doubt. Although we said you will have to be the final judge, this certainly does not prohibit you from seeking expert counsel during the process. In fact, advice is urgently indicated. The superb service your management development specialist can offer you lies in the array of alternatives he can spread out for your inspection. His training and experience make him especially sympathetic to your needs, and he will have great empathy for your situation. By all means, lean heavily on his expertise.

The second step in this process has already been mentioned, but is in need of reinforcement. That is the necessity for your unalterable determination to let nothing interfere with carrying out your program. The most widespread human frailty is interruptibility. All of us tend to be sidetracked from a major objective by the minor irritants of daily life. You must put yourself above these, and drive toward the important goal. Possibly the enactment of this determination may be noted by others as a personality change in you, as indeed it may be. Whatever the costs in disturbed interpersonal relationships, your end result will make it worthwhile, and your real friends will not be permanently estranged by your new behavior. Your newly acquired firmness will elicit more admiration than it will frustration or anger among your associates. Their respect for you will grow.

Is Your Program Functional?

No development program is worth its salt unless it is completely functional. This means that as each strength or technique is developed, it must be immediately built into your work on a continuing basis. These applications are needed to confirm your learning, and to increase your effectiveness on the job. Remember that the installation of each of these tools should also have a payoff in greater efficiency, with a concomitant saving of time. Moreover, this time will be discretionary, and will free you for further developmental activity.

It should be apparent by now that the most important single aspect of your development program is to determine whether a proposed element is remedial, or is actually leading you into a different and untried field. The flexing of muscles already well along in their development must be left to your habitual responses. You will not have the time to concentrate on them consciously. If this sounds as if we are laying out a Spartan existence for you, you are correct. Being chosen for middle management is one of the true separations of the men from the boys you will experience in your lifetime.

Obviously, you must remain calm during this period. The conservation of your total energy is of ultimate importance; you have no justification for any side trips down diverting pathways now. As a self-protective measure, you should again reevaluate your personal set of controls to be sure that they offer maximum protection of your time. This must be done without sacrifice of your personal relationships with your associates, *but it must be done.* Those about you will recognize your new posture and purpose, and will have much understanding of the rigors you are undergoing. They are prepared to be sympathetic, as long as you make reasonable efforts to be decent to them. After all, they are members of the select group, too.

Where Were You a Year Ago?

If you are really a candidate for promotion to middle management, you were probably in the same job a year ago that you are in today, so this question is basically unfair. That is not the intent. We are inquiring about how much growth and development you have undergone in that period of time—most of it probably simply on the job, or in purely job-related activities. The amount of growth a person experiences in a given year is the product of several variables. If it is his first year on that job, the development should be greater than it will be in any other year until he is again promoted. If he has been in the same position for many years, it is natural enough that the rate-of-growth curve will decrease sharply, until finally it loses its curvature altogether, and becomes a straight line.

This matter of comparing your position today with that of a year ago is an important undertaking in itself, because it gives you excellent practice in introspection, which should be an ongoing part of your professional life. However, for this measurement to be valid, you will have to establish some standards in various areas against which to plot your improvements. These should be as literal and pragmatic as you can make them. If your last year's diagnosis showed you needed a plus in your interpersonal relationships, it would have been logical for you to have set a percentage reduction in grievances in your crew as a target for this element. Or, if you want to live dangerously, as a subsidiary target in this facet you might have aimed for a percentage reduction in rejection of your production by quality control inspectors, under the general thesis that at least a part of their paperhanging may have originated in poor relationships between your group and the inspectors.

Another clear benefit from this process is that the knowledge you are acquiring will be functional when you get seriously into Management by Objectives. The way the trend is going, that should be soon after your promotion into middle management. It is a way of life which will become nearly inevitable for every manager, since its overall objective approach takes so much of the sting and personality abrasion out of the process of management. Why not do it the easy way, if it is the best?

Another moving standard against which you might measure your accomplishments is that of your peers' growth during the same period of time. This comparison is an especially valuable method if some of them are performing the same function you are. Since their criteria are identical, the comparison of two, three, or four first-line production foremen can give you extremely valuable insight, especially if they report to the same second- or third-line manager. A forced choice between two peers is a standard statistical procedure of great value. Furthermore, it may reveal weaknesses in one individual which had escaped detection in a general survey of his accomplishments against inanimate standards. This is a plus.

There must be demonstrable progress and development over each year's time. You cannot afford to stand still at this stage in your career. In fact, there can be no such thing as standing still. You will either progress or regress, since others are running hard in the same race, and you will never lack for stiff competition. You can't even get tired—or show it.

You will recognize, of course, that much of the measurement of your growth will be by indirect method; that is, by putting the gauges to your crew, rather than to yourself. Since your job is now to get your work done through other people, you must measure their accomplishments in order to get at your own performance. To carry this to the extreme, your progress may be related on a one-to-one basis by your management with theirs. Your first reaction to this concept may be to brand it as highly unfair, but it is not. This *is* the measure of the inactive leader of the group.

This procedure, important as it is to you, is going to take a massive impartial monitoring in order to be valid and reliable. At this juncture, do not trust your unsup-

WHAT IS THE STATE OF YOUR DEVELOPMENT PLAN?

ported judgment of your situation. You must already have guessed the two people recommended to give you this service: your superior, and the management development specialist, or his equivalent. In effect, determination of your status will become a committee affair. This is good. It will call for the highest degree of objectivity from all of you, and there will be built-in controls for accuracy of observation and honesty of reportage. Both of these are important. The most important benefit of the group effort is your opportunity to develop and implement a completely workable development program for the next time period. Nothing must impede this progress, since time now becomes more critical each year.

By good planning, and a calculated effort by the three of you, you can guarantee that no year of your current career will show a plateau in development. Plateaus are not allowed. (Fifteen years' experience, or one year's experience repeated fourteen times?) The greatest benefit which can result from this cooperative effort will be a conditioning—a habituating—to the entire process of self-development. Once it has sunk to this level of your consciousness, much of the trauma will be removed from its smooth and easy continuation. It is mandatory that you build this process into your work life in such a manner that it does not interfere with your daily routine. We all know the tremendous accumulation of detail which has dogged your footsteps ever since your entry into supervision. The ultimate goal, of course, is the ability to concentrate, without distraction, on the achievement of the current goals, and to plan concurrently for future expansion. The two must go hand in hand.

What Are Your Greatest Needs for Growth?

If you are deeply committed to succeed in your ambition to be promoted to middle management, something must be done to bolster up your weak spots and to present a more symmetrical picture to your competition and to your management. The logical approach will be to assign priorities to these needs, and to attack them on that basis. For example, you have known for years that you have difficulty in oral communication when more than two or three people are in the group. Your boss has indicated, both formally and informally, that he would be delighted to have you make a presentation to his manager's staff meeting on any facet of your job you might choose. For one reason or another, you have never accepted these repeated invitations. The whole prospect fills you with horror, and you know the result would be a complete disaster. But that is only a recognition of a major problem, with no attempt to do something about it. You are a big boy now, and the next move is yours. Your boss is not about to order you to take remedial steps in a nebulous area. The solution is obvious. A year in a toastmasters' club might work wonders for your self-confidence and your ability to communicate orally.

Maybe the major problem is a lack of sensitivity to the fine shades of meanings shown by those with whom you communicate. Perhaps you listen only to what they say, and not to what they don't say. Your preoccupation with your total job keeps you from concentrating on what others are sending for your reception; your decoding is imperfect and incomplete. We now have a new tool for probing and correcting this weakness: sensitivity training. It is a rough sort of therapy, and you may regret ever having engaged in it, but if you approach it in an adult frame of mind, it may be quite a turning point in your life. Some people in management have completely reversed abrasive interpersonal relationships as a result of this specialized training. Since you are in a position of leadership, you must remember that a change in signal from you will have a disturbing effect on your subordinates. They will require a reasonable period in which to adjust to the new you.

How about your technical expertise? It is more than probable that you are supervising more than one trade or discipline. Have you gone on for a year or more without making a serious effort to become at least superficially familiar with a work classification new to you? No one will force you to dig into this. You are on your own. The matter of face should never become a consideration. You will undoubtedly gain the respect and prestige of the employees when they see you learning how to communicate with them in their own field.

When your self-analysis has identified areas which need attention, the procedure should be perfectly clear. You will evolve a plan for corrective action, and then implement that plan posthaste. The key is the maturity of your outlook. You can grow and develop only when you satisfy felt needs. Your perception has to be actively involved in the entire sequence, or there can be no real learning.

Your response to this basic situation will be one of the significant determinants of your future career. You are picking an extremely delicate course through a quagmire. One false step on either side of the line will either delay you seriously, or be the death knell of your future in management.

The foregoing has been more negative than is healthy for your perspective. During the process of identifying and applying first aid to your weaknesses, you should not overlook at least ancillary care and feeding of your stronger indicators. They will need minimal watching to maintain their health. You are the moderator of this continuing action.

Right now it could be profitable to recheck the perspective of your job in its entirety. You are the core of an action which affects many other people. Involved are your management, your peers, and your subordinates. As you change, so will your relationships with them. Maybe your greatest growth need at present is a reevaluation of your multigroup memberships on the job. You must be willing to be more flexible in adjusting to *their* reactions to your change. The onus is on you to prevent your associates from becoming seriously upset. Your one overriding responsibility is the best for the most. When this is put in jeopardy by an action of yours, you must be the one prepared to take corrective steps. It is not fair to allow others to suffer from your desire for progress. The fact that you will be put into the same position by their developmental activities is not germane. In that case, of course, they will be the ones forced to adjust.

This give-and-take among the group is one of the more delicate educative processes that results from membership in management. It is a civilizing influence in what otherwise is a jungle. Your basic procedure having been outlined, the rest is up to you. You make your anlaysis; you develop a plan; you implement it; you evaluate results. The process of maturation is always painful. You can expect growing pains throughout your managerial career exactly as you had them in your youth. The side effect upon your feelings will be uncomfortable, but you can learn to live with it if you keep your eye on the objective of well-rounded development.

Now Where Do You Go for Help?

During this search for resources in your development, you must remember that you are considerably more sophisticated than you were when you were preparing for entry into supervision. Some of the source material will still be useful, but only as a review and refresher rather than as actual learning material. You are going to have to go further and deeper to satisfy your needs.

Experts tell us that 90 percent of all growth and development occurs right on the job. This means that you, and no one else, can put to your advantage those things which happen daily at work. It is a matter of being aware of what is going on in a special way, with reference to its usefulness for you. Man has, unfortunately, a great ability to remain unconscious of the things closest to him in his environment. The other side of the coin is for you deliberately to design and make things happen which will stretch you and enrich your experience. If carefully thought out, these special projects can be of immense value both to you and to the organization. Included would be special studies of method or layout, experimental work procedures leading toward increased efficiency and lower costs, new organizational structures intended to streamline your operations, and many other projects which only you will be in a position to conceptualize.

The main intent during this period will be to build your group (and your job) into a more functional and smoothly running engine. You will be engineering your own transition from lower-level supervision to middle management. Until you receive your actual promotion, you must get vicarious experience as a middle manager in your current position.

Ordinarily, you should expect to get the best cooperation from your superior, since everything you will be planning and doing will be to his advantage and to that of the enterprise. The one major limitation which will be imposed is that you must not do anything which will have a major effect on the operation of any of your peers without their complete understanding and agreement. No conscientious manager can expect to impose change on others unilaterally. But again, in most instances you will find your peers receptive to change if they can see a possible benefit either to themselves or to the organization. They may even be willing to go along through pure friendship and the desire to be of help. One extremely important point to keep in mind at all times is: Keep a complete record of your plans and their implementation. Those responsible for your advancement will need reassurance that these events were planned, rather than the happy result of chance.

We said 90 percent of your development would be job related. That does not mean that the other 10 percent is unimportant. On the contrary, some of it will make most significant contributions to your growth as a manager. Now is the time to profit from an outside seminar, for example. You have a background of managerial experience which can be related meaningfully to the content discussed at the meetings. You will be able to evaluate what you hear from other members of the group, and pick and choose from their ideas. Just about now you should hold serious conversations with your superior and the management development specialist in your organization. Offerings in the field of developmental experiences are proliferating like jackrabbits these days. Their literature is appearing in a veritable flood; choosing among the offerings is difficult unless you are experienced, and culling the good from the bad takes expertise.

There are, in general, two criteria to help you judge which of the seminars might be useful to you. The first criterion relates to the firm presenting the seminar. There is a small, select list of universities and agencies whose seminars are especially reliable. Your management development man will know about them, and will also be of help in deciding which ones would be most valuable for you. The second criterion is based on the names of the conference leaders. Some of the best available men work alone; their offerings will be limited in number, but of a high degree of excellence. It may be difficult to get into their seminars, and you should be willing to plan ahead for as long as a year, if necessary, to be admitted to a desired workshop. One caution should be observed here: After they have achieved eminence, these people sometimes take on assistants in order to multiply their revenue. The second men may or may not be as good as the principal. The best procedure is to check the experience of a friend or acquaintance who has attended one of these meetings.

A word about general procedure in going to outside seminars: For best results, you must cooperate completely with the suggestions they make and must totally immerse yourself in the experience, even to the exclusion of any contact with your job while they are in progress. You will find demands on your time and energy running up to twelve or fourteen hours a day during the scheduled time of the meeting. You simply will not have enough minutes to get the most from the seminar and also to be in touch with your office. You should be prepared to delegate complete responsibility and authority to a good assistant, and literally to forget your job for the duration of the developmental experience. (For this reason, many seminars are held in country clubs far from any metropolitan center. Even telephone calls coming to you may be screened.) Besides, your boss will still be available to keep a fatherly eye on your area during your absence. This complete concentration will multiply many times the benefit you gain from the experience.

What Is Your Time Schedule?

Your personal ambition and the pressures you feel from each advancing year naturally bias your answer to this question. Of course you would like whatever development is essential for promotion to take place instantaneously, so that you could start to drum on management's door. To be more realistic, however, we must point out a time increment will be involved for the complete implementation of your development program. Nothing could be so disruptive as to try to rush any part of it. The whole process is one of maturation, and we all know that a slowly maturing organism is sounder than one which puffs up, but is hollow inside. One point is undeniable: The job of the middle manager can be handled successfully only by a mature individual. The daily work requires too much judgment to depend on the callow personality. In fact, one major objective of a development program is expedition of the ripening process. Perhaps it is not so much expediting as streamlining. Unguided and unplanned growth will be both asymmetrical and slower to occur than one which is the product of planning and design.

Minimal time limits can be set with some definiteness for certain kinds of development programs. For example, you should never enter a toastmasters' club and expect to get optimal results in less than a year. You will achieve much more if you allow two years for this activity. Some proprietary seminars, such as those offered by Kepner-Tregoe, are designed with follow-up extending over a three- or six-month period. Sloan fellowships normally run for an academic year of nine months. Many other seminars have similar time requirements. Almost any outside effort worth the time and money you expend should be given an indefinite period of time so that you can assimilate the content fully and begin to work it into your job routine.

You have a good deal of control over the timing of most of your development program. The trick is to make your very best judgment of how much time is needed for the completion of each facet, and then to discipline yourself so that you adhere rigidly to this minimal schedule, recognizing that for the most part it will result in a better final product. The way to save time is through meticulous programming as a whole, fitting the pieces together to blend with your job, your home life, and other demands in the most efficient manner. It would be well to carry over one technique from formal schooling—the allotment of liberal time for review and recapitulation at regularly scheduled intervals. This technique will do as much as anything else to ensure an overall quality product.

However, don't hesitate to ask for the appraisals and judgments of qualified observers on the results you are getting. Impartial rating of your effort by others will help immensely in clearing your own perspective. Ask for, and accept, their most rigorous analyses of both your methods and your results in the developmental area. One group who most certainly should not be forgotten in this connection are your subordinates. Never let your pride interfere with getting their opinions about your endeavors in self-development. Their position in the hierarchy makes them peculiarly adept at judging your results and progress. Be completely open in seeking their estimates and advice.

Both stimulation and frustration will be associated with this period in your career. The excitement of discovering and mastering new disciplines will be balanced by your anxiety to see the payoff. This will be a major test of your patience and ability to live with stress. Hopefully, if your program has been well designed and faithfully executed, some positive gains will not be long in coming.

* * *

This chapter may have disturbed—even irritated—you because the subject matter seemed vaguely familiar, and well it should. You were asked to recycle the process by which you gained admission into the ranks of supervision, but at a higher and more complex level. The elements are the same generically, but they are more sophisticated and intricate in their achievement.

First, it is entirely possible that you may have forgotten

the existence of development plans because of your deep involvement with the details of supervisory life. The rediscovery of the concept itself may be painful to you.

Next, you will have to make some value judgments about whether your efforts are truly constructive, or whether you are attempting to cover up glaring weaknesses rather than turning them into strengths. At that point, you should look back and compare your present position to that of a year ago. This is often humiliating. As a result of that exercise, you must assign priorities to your developmental needs on the basis of their urgency in your present and projected performance. You will be gratified to discover that an overpowering majority of your efforts will be job associated, and that only a tiny (but important) fraction of them will take you off the work area for their satisfaction.

7

What Evidence Do You Have of Your Promotability?

MANY organizations which use a ranking system for rating their supervisors cloak the entire process in the deepest secrecy. That is the pleasant illusion under which they operate. Actually, only rarely do the supervisors involved not know their relative rank on the totem pole. They all develop their pipelines among clerks and secretaries, because these general salaried personnel have access to what is theoretically classified information. Naturally, your place on the list is highly important in connection with your hopes for another promotion.

However, it is not necessary that you be in the number-one position for you to get the next advancement. Many other considerations go into each promotion. Perhaps there are some special aspects in the department where the vacancy is, and management might decide that your personality and qualifications would exactly fill the bill, even if you were rated number three or four on the list. It goes without saying, however, that you must be well above the midpoint in order to be considered for promotion, except in times of the wildest boom and the most profuse growth in the organization.

At this point there arises the question of consonance between your philosophy and that of upper management. We have worked under the general assumption that you have been as objective as possible in creating and administering your development program. Hopefully, upper management promotes its supervisors into middle management on at least as objective a basis. If there is any vestige of whimsical or intuitive selection of nominees, you are at best playing Russian roulette with your chances for advancement. Happily, the general trend in American management is moving clearly toward Management by Objectives, with its absolute dependence on objectivity of approach. In fact, only a minimum of digging on your part should expose the general nature of the criteria used to promote supervisors into middle management. It should not be necessary to dwell on obvious considerations such as production, quality, sales, and costs. Neither should we have to reinforce too strongly the emphasis which will be put on your relationships with labor and employees.

Nevertheless, it would be misleading not to point out that some factors in promotions are necessarily highly subjective. These, fortunately, are ordinarily used as tie breakers. For example, the candidate with the better personality may be picked over a competitor who is his equal in all other respects, or the man with a full record of community activity will be chosen over a rival who has zeroed in only on work experience.

Because there is no surefire way of knowing when these subjective attributes will become major determinants of promotion, we must return to the overriding importance of your position on the totem pole. All other things being equal, if you are riding high and are indisputably in the number-one position, you will have an almost impregnable advantage over your competitors. It is also pleasant to note that you can take deliberate aim at the top spot with a reasonable chance for success if you do your planning conscientiously, and work diligently at achieving your developmental targets. As we said, only in the most devious and dishonest of managements are promotional criteria kept secret. Once you have the criteria in your possession, the rest is nearly automatic. We should reemphasize the importance of persistence and stamina. More promotions are won by default of lazy candidates than by incontrovertible superiority of the winner.

Do You Know Your Competition?

From the foregoing, you can see how important it is to size up your competition with clarity and competence. The winner of any race knows both the faults and the strengths of his rivals. He gives due respect to them when it is deserved, and gears his own efforts to outdo them, if possible, but at least decides to settle for no less than a tie. In his weaknesses, you can assume that you will be clearly ahead—unless they are the same as your own.

Preparing a physical chart of available candidates in promotional standards could be of real service to your race. You should use a scale which will allow a visual comparison of all the characteristics of all the candidates. A composite summary for each one should then be put on the same type of scale. By this method, the areas on which you need to concentrate especially will be clearly visible. It might be wise at this point to cut your time increment in half, and make these summary comparisons every three months rather than semi-annually. You are in the position of the racehorse who is called upon to make his greatest effort in the approach to the wire.

We hope we have not given the impression of making the developmental process a mechanical thing. It is based entirely on human attributes and human activity; only the measurements of this work can be mechanized for purposes of comparison. The challenge of making a run for advancement to middle management is no greater (if as great) as that which you underwent in making the jump into supervision. Only the techniques and methodology become more complex. Of course, we are not underestimating the fact that your competitors are sharper and more alert than those you faced in the previous round. Of paramount importance is the matter of keeping your head, and refusing to be panicked by the actions either of others seeking the new job or of upper management as you interpret their behavior during the selection process. The activities of either group can be extremely misleading when seen from your biased viewpoint.

What Is Your Status Among Your Peers?

Status among professional people has to be earned. It has little to do with the artificial value which employees often attach to position in the hierarchy. The opinion your fellow supervisors hold of you will be a composite of several factors. First, they evaluate (partly for personal and selfish reasons) your integrity. This goes a long way beyond an estimation of your fiscal honesty. They are more concerned about how you interact with them on the job. Are you honest both with them and about them? Can they depend on your word, once given, even if the situation should become uncomfortable for you? Of course, the unforgivable sin would be for you to abandon them in a touchy spot to save your own skin. This evaluation of your integrity does not come swiftly, but must be forged from some clearly defined and visible incidents. Not every one of your associates will have to be personally involved in such events; however, there must be one incident on the basis of which they can give judgment.

Second, your peers will form an opinion about your technical competence on the job. They will not expect you to be a journeyman in each of the crafts or disciplines represented in your crew, but they will judge you on your ability to appraise the work of your subordinates properly. In their eyes, a major part of your technical competence will become evident by the smoothness with which you can meet your deadlines against the natural roadblocks that always appear. They will watch with special care your reaction to delays and mistakes in other departments which have an effect on your operation. The twin brother to this facet of your status is your willingness to cooperate with them, especially when it may cause you some upset. In fact, there will be some deviously engineered tests of your cooperation early in your association with them.

Third, your peers will render a separate judgment on your ability in interpersonal relationships in every direction and in all your contacts. Perhaps the closest scrutiny will be given to how you approach your subordinates, since they are well aware that it is to your advantage to get along well with peers and superiors. On the other hand, you will be severely criticized should they decide that you are soft on your people. A fine line of demarcation is drawn in determination of good or bad human skills.

Fourth, some elements of status are much less definitive than those mentioned so far. Your peers will be deeply interested in your ability to ride with the punches thrown at you by top management. Rigidity in the face of the inevitable is not always considered a virtue. To measure up in their eyes, you must be able to make swift and complete adjustment to forced changes in your plans. They feel comfortable if they find you flexible, since this ability can possibly be turned to their advantage in the future.

This analysis of your status among your peers would be incomplete if we failed to recognize their search for charisma in your demonstrated leadership. They will not be too visibly disappointed if they fail to find it, but evidences of its presence will boost your stock by many points. In all probability, they will not even verbalize on this element, but it will go into their personal computers as a part of the final printout.

A significant part of your peers' final evaluation of the esteem you deserve will be generated by conversations among themselves about you. This living in a goldfish bowl will have to become a recognized part of your life in modern management. It is not a new facet of the process of living, but it will be intensified as you enter middle management, and will continue to grow as you climb the ladder. The sooner you adjust to it, the better you will feel.

While this process is under way, you should be looking for inputs from your peers, and keeping a rough, but functional, computation of how you rate. There should be no vanity or ego involvement about this. It is of purely practical importance to you and your career that you have the good opinion of the majority of your peers. All of us know of managers who have risen to the top surrounded by the cordial hatred of everyone they know. These things do happen, but they are extremely rare, and only serve to accentuate the fact that the rise is accomplished against nearly insuperable odds. Those managers who do pull off this feat do so because of other rich endowments in critical aspects requisite for success. Their accomplishments underline how much value may be derived from earning high status among your peers.

To summarize: Your status will evolve from your normal daily activity. In some respects you have little control over it, because an adult's behavior pattern is set so firmly that it takes a Herculean effort to change it markedly. Although you must be aware of what is going on, you must not be pressured by the knowledge that you are building a reputation day by day among your peers. This is as natural as the fact that you are also forming opinions of them, individually and collectively. Your first act should be to pull out the wiring of your panic button, and remove forever the temptation to push it when things seem to be going wrong. Although character and reputation are not necessarily positively correlated, they might just as well be so far as the results on your future are concerned. In the business world, you are what you appear to be among your associates.

How Do Your People Feel About You?

The good will of your peer group is important to you; it is at least as urgent that your subordinates be well disposed toward you when you are trying for another promotion. Once in management, you can look no better than your group. Their production, quality, sales, and costs will be yours. Certainly, if they like and respect you, they will go that little step further at times to make you look good. You need not set out formally to measure your status with your people. In fact, if you did so, you would without question get some badly skewed readings from some of them. They would be either resentful or embarrassed by having you approach them directly about such a personal matter as their regard for you.

Nevertheless, there are barometers which will give you an accurate total reading of your status in the group. For example, what is the incidence of grievances or complaints in your work area? More important, through how many steps of the grievance procedure is the average complaint by one of your people processed? A second, equally good indicator is your safety index. Irritated and frustrated employees are more accident prone than those whose feelings are in the normal range. Your severity rate will be higher as your popularity decreases. Obviously, people neither allow accidents to happen to themselves on purpose nor willfully incur a more serious one. These occurrences are the result of the distraught condition of disgruntled and unhappy workers.

Almost always concurrent with an ominous rise in grievances and accidents will be a drop-off in the number of suggestions turned in by your group, either formally or informally. A much more intangible and hard-to-measure standard is the activity of the rumor mill in your jurisdictional sphere. Times of upset or uncertainty will lead to the production of more and sturdier rumors.

We can generalize from this last statement and say that in the crew enjoying normal to good relationships with its supervisor, communications of all sorts will flow more freely than they do when those relationships are poor. One of the first signs of dislike between two individuals is in an unwillingness to talk to each other. Odd as it may seem, the better your people like you, and the higher your status with them, the more willing they will be to pass on bad news. It is the boss who is feared or hated who never hears anything but good news from his area. Nevertheless, a significant part of your estimate of how you stand with your people must be intuitive. You will take your readings on all available indicators, put them into your personal computer, and then use your intuition to meld them into one overall estimate. This is a fairly ordinary managerial decision-making technique.

By all means, you should make a sincere effort to check your findings against the estimates your peers have of your status with your people. Your peers are much less biased in their observations than you can ever hope to be, and many times will be able to get information your people would never reveal to you directly. On either a tacit or a spoken understanding of the necessity for reciprocity, you can get good cooperation from your opposite numbers in this kind of research. The necessity for occasional mutual back scratching is as evident among managers as among any other segment of the population. You should not have any reason for hesitating to use the services of your peers. Actually, it might be in order to offer to do an informal survey in their areas simultaneously with their activity in yours. They will be at least as interested in your results as you are in theirs.

Unless your superior is quite unusual and highly unorthodox, he will be of small help in gathering these data. The only thing he can do is to get them to pass you as they go downward in the line, and both of you should frown on this procedure, if for no other reason than that it will make your subordinates uncomfortable.

One small thunderhead lies far on the horizon in connection with this exercise. That is the hopefully remote danger that you will become hypnotized by the fascinating details, and overdo the process to the ultimate damage of the status you first set out to measure. The tolerance of people for this kind of close observation of personality is notoriously low. They tend to react with sudden irritation if they feel the probing has been overextended. The word "backlash" is entirely descriptive of their possible reaction. Your group status is a curious mixture of individual inputs which are then summed up and modified by further group processing. Your people talk about you at great length. This is part of the life of the supervisor. Modifications of personal opinions will naturally occur during the interactions between various members of the group who have great respect for each other's views. Thus, we have a good illustration of the fact that the group is greater than the sum of its individual parts.

The final conclusions of the group about your status will be closely representative of the individual thinking of its members, with the exception of small percentages at either extreme of the normal bell curve of distribution. Thus, an impartial observer could take a random sampling of 15 or 20 percent of your crew and give you a reliably accurate estimate of where you stand with your subordinates. This might be the least disturbing way for you to make your survey. The resultant disturbance would be minimal, and you would still have a fine chance to make a correct reading.

Are You Clean Administratively?

It is easy to lose yourself in the routines and minor emergencies of daily living. You can overlook the fact that management up the line keeps a special set of books on your performance which you never see. The entries in these ledgers include some items you would consider insignificant, and other major observations of which you may not even be aware. For example, how good are you in getting your routine report upstairs on time? Do you keep all the loose ends tied on every grievance active in your area? When special information, not generally sent upstairs, is requested, how quickly and accurately do you respond? The fact that you are given no information, not even the courtesy of generalities about the need for these responses, has nothing to do with your responsibility for delivering the required data. Your scores in these incidents can be

WHAT EVIDENCE DO YOU HAVE OF YOUR PROMOTABILITY?

decisive in determining whether you will be promoted. They are critical. The current thinking among the higher-ups is that the attention you give these special details are direct indicators of your managerial sensitivity and conceptual skills. And, after all, the executives *do* make the rules.

Another set of entries will certainly be made about your errors of commission, or omission, concerning company policy. You are not required to agree while at the first level; but you are required to see that policy is put into effect easily and smoothly. Failure to set the wheels in motion concerning a new administrative procedure is the easiest way to get into strong disfavor with the kingmakers. *This is not the time to take them on in a test of strength.* You do that in areas where their ego involvement is less apparent, and where, if they fail, losing face is not a factor.

Parenthetically, we should remind ourselves of the semantic sea we are adrift in when we use the words "management," "supervision," and "administration." It is obvious that we are including the supervisor as a part of management *in all aspects of his job,* although admittedly this is not the approach used everywhere in the real world. We use the word "administration" to mean a *subfunction of management.* Again, in the real world, the title "administrator" sometimes is higher than "manager," but more often the reverse is true. Your discrimination must be utilized here.

Remember that you are responsible for the administrative record not only for yourself, but for your crew as well. This is especially obvious in the innumerable requirements in the matter of personnel records. Even if the requests come to the individuals concerned, *you* will receive the demerits if the information is not forthcoming punctually. Since there is the distinct possibility that you may not be aware of some of the paperwork involved, it is good procedure to check routinely on a timed basis to see that all clerical records for your people are up to date. These records can be of life-or-death importance. You are the control agent for their proper forwarding and entering into the records. *Keep all records clean.*

You must also be sensitive to the information you give your boss which is important to his personal record. He has the same overriding responsibility for you that you have for your subordinates. His only chance for making a good record is to have all the facts told to him promptly and completely. Your empathy must be employed in sending him the necessary information. You can swamp your boss with an avalanche of reports; you can scuttle him irretrievably if you fail to give him all the necessary parts of the puzzle.

One feature of administrative detail is the record you keep of your contacts with other departments and functions. The interweaving of different work groups becomes so complex that no middle manager can possibly remember the interfaces without clean reporting from each of his staff members. In one sense, these contacts have greater influence on you and on your boss's future than do activities in your own direct line. Executive management depend for their successful operation on complete data from every element of the complex. The need for getting a clear picture of liaison work within the group increases sharply when the organization is a matrix. The greater number of individual contacts, and the matter of reporting to many bosses instead of one, make much more composite the delineation of a complete and clear picture of activities. Not to know what is going on is, of course, the kiss of death to any manager's career.

Build administrative details into your daily routine by a judicious use of controls. Remind yourself of repetitive reports by means of your tickler file—or, better still, be sure that your clerk or secretary does this. They should be making the reports, of course. Acquire keen sensitivity about the necessity for "special information" so often casually tossed over the shoulder at you by a harried superior. He will assume you can see its importance; it is your duty to respond quickly and accurately.

In acquiring a good sense of administrative detail, you will be undergoing admirable development in the conceptual skills which will start to loom as urgent when you enter middle management. The widening of your perspective, and of your appreciation for many more fine details and how they fit into the mosaic, will mature you rapidly as a manager. We have already stressed the importance of maturity in the life of the middle manager.

There are a few more segments in the summation of your estimate of readiness for promotion, but by now you should have a nearly complete concept of what you are up against in the next echelon. Things will be both more detailed and wider along the spectrum. This apparent dichotomy must be rationalized before you can make your necessary decisions. So, let's get ahead with the job.

How Are Your Contacts with the Front Office?

Before you can consider your chance for promotion into middle management as at all significant, you will have to make repeated contacts with middle and upper management. All other things being equal, the man who gets the promotion will be the one who is personally known to the executive echelon. We all trust someone we know more than we trust a stranger. You will have to depend on your own resources to contrive many more of these contacts than would come about normally between a first- or second-line supervisor and the functional executives.

One of the better ways to make some of these meetings occur without being too obvious is to volunteer for some of the special projects which are always floating around in any organization. Your supervisor could probably name three or four things he would like to have done which fit into no one's specific job duties. If he is normally thoughtful, he will hesitate to assign any of these projects to subordinates he knows are already running hard. Therefore, a prime way to get his goodwill and to come to the notice of upper management is to volunteer to take on one of these special jobs. In addition to the purely selfish objective already mentioned, the pursuit of the information necessary for the completion of the desired report will add to your general or special knowledge of the company's operation.

Nearly all companies of any size contain semiformal organizations of their management divided into supervisors' clubs or management associations. They may range from purely social groups to study groups, or combinations of these two across the spectrum. In any event, they have the official or semiofficial blessing of top management, and officers of the management club are better known than others at their level. Getting yourself involved in political activity here will bring your name before the management group, whether or not you are successful in becoming an officer of it. It will also serve the purpose of widening noticeably your acquaintanceship among your peers.

A more obvious, but a little more difficult, way to become noticed by top management is to force some contacts outside the job area. You may decide to seek membership in a particular lodge, church, or private club because you know several key executives from your enterprise are members. Because this method is quite obvious to most people, you will have to handle the situation with special care, or it might backfire. You may even want to give the appearance of avoiding contacts with these people in your new group. If you seem to lean over backward not to curry favor, no censure can be attached to your new membership, and eventually things can be allowed to take their natural course. You may have more contacts than you desired in the first place.

Another unimpeachable way of multiplying your contacts with the Olympians is to go through channels to get from a specific executive some information you need for your own operation. This approach can never be criticized. It is especially applicable when you are planning for a possible innovation, and need figures and facts not currently in your possession in order to come to a decision. Even if the final decision to introduce the new idea is negative, you will have accomplished your basic purpose.

There is one frustrating aspect to this entire campaign. No matter how many meetings, accidental or otherwise, you achieve with top management, the feedback you get about their reaction will be too little to satisfy you. Any reactions you do get from them will be deviously indirect.

A friend in another area may report casually that he recently had a conversation about you with one of your executives, but don't expect much in the way of content. The fact that you were the subject of a conversation is in itself significant.

There is, of course, one source quite near who can be of value to you—your own boss. If his interest in your advancement is positive, he will be actively looking for ways to increase your visibility upstairs, and will also be in a much better position to evaluate your impact there once you have made some appearances. He will get direct feedback from his superiors on any official activity in which you have been engaged with executive row, since this is material which will certainly be used by your superior in his reviews of your performance.

Perhaps the most dangerous method of all is to try to involve your wife in your political affairs. She will normally have social contacts with the wives of many other managers in your company; company people are usually encouraged to socialize frequently among their own group. The laws of probability could easily turn up some important contacts through your wife's socializing, but to follow them through for hidden self-serving purposes is a dangerous tactic. The other husbands involved by their wives in what is obviously a kind of cabal will predictably react with some violence, and your cause might in the long run suffer severe damage. Of course, this game is by its very nature perilous to you. Your action is now on the edges of the big time; you have served your apprenticeship in the minor leagues, and are understandably anxious to try out in the majors. Essentially, the people concerned will understand and allow for this desire, and they are not going to fault you too severely for making the run. It is only the methods you use which can often cause heavily critical comments.

What Is the Addition?

Hopefully, by this time you have completed a fair survey of your position and your present chances for advancement. If you have found some gaps in your armor, your course is clearly defined. They should be closed at once. However, you should remember that in all probability no one has ever been perfectly ready for a promotion when it came his way. Everyone has areas in which he wishes he could improve, and every manager who wants to remain competitive must continually be working on his own development. The real value of an introspective summary of your position is to make you completely aware of the job that lies ahead. You cannot expect to go at it blindly and come up with viable results.

The second good result of your study will be the instant summation you can give your superior during a performance review. He may know well every point you bring out, but he will be deeply concerned that you have self-knowledge and understanding of your relative strengths and weaknesses. On the other hand, you may remind him of things which have slipped his mind, and so give him a more complete picture than he would otherwise have had.

The importance to you of a well-rounded development cannot be emphasized too strongly. The middle manager is, indeed, the man in the middle. His balance must be well-nigh perfect, or he will be toppled by the first heavy attack on his position. The basis of his strength must be self-confidence, and this can come only from knowledge of good preparation.

Another consideration should be mentioned: the danger inherent in being promoted too far too soon. We have all seen the catastrophes which can occur when this happens. It can lead to the complete ruin of a person who had great potential; once his confidence is gone, and others have seen his inadequate performance, he may never get a chance to repair the damages. This downfall is caused by the unhappy meeting of two errors: One is management's miscalculation of the candidate's state of readiness; and the other, the misperception of the man of his own preparedness. The failure usually occurs when there has been inadequate communication among the various echelons, especially those centering at the first or second level, where the nominee is ready for action. There can be no excuse for this event.

The most common reason for the tragedy of too fast a promotion is an insufficient briefing of the supervisor on the real requirements of the middle management job. He may be unaware of the greater depths of knowledge required and the speedier action normal in the big time. He may be terrified, and then hypnotized, by a sudden realization of the importance of the decisions he will have to make daily. The greater magnitude of the money involved, and the larger numbers of people whose futures are in his care, may combine in a one-two blow to put him on the ropes if he has not been properly prepared.

Assuredly, this discussion was not meant to cause you to develop an inferiority complex, but if you do, perhaps you would be less than happy as a middle manager anyway. The difference between being stretched by your job, and being broken on the wheel by it, is one of those maddeningly thin lines with which we all have to learn to live. So we come full circle back to the inescapable conclusion that you can prevent failure by the simple procedure of being sure you are ready for an advancement before you take it on. The length of preparation will be determined by your present state, your ability to learn, your reserves of strength which will allow you to take on extra work when you are already running under a full head of steam, and the sagacity of the counseling you receive from your supervisor and those above him in the line. Each of these factors must be accounted for; each must contribute its part to your next big step forward.

* * *

This chapter has been a homing-in device to help you assess your readiness for promotion into middle management. One of the bench marks, certainly, is your position on the totem pole—where you rate in comparison with your peers and opposite numbers. In addition, you must have the full trust and confidence of *all* who work with you, including superiors, peers, and subordinates. There must be positive action beyond trust, however, in the shape of adequate cooperation given and received. No one person today can accomplish a full job in business or industry. We are too interwoven and interdependent to be lone performers ever again.

You must be certain that you have kept good marks in the administrative parts of your job, for upper management will be fussy in this area. They want the records complete and clear. Above and beyond this record, you must make a series of personal contacts with executives, so that they can get to know you and be able to evaluate you on the basis of this personal knowledge. Seldom will they agree to the promotion of an unknown into the middle management ranks. Most of these contacts will have to be made at your contrivance, yet they must not be too obvious. Your boss can help you here.

Finally, you must summarize in your own thinking your exact position at this moment in time, and be satisfied in your own mind that you are truly ready to go higher up the pyramid.

8

How Are Your Peer Relationships?

How many friends do you have on the job? This can be an embarrassing question—not because you will necessarily count a large number of enemies, but because it is often difficult to assess exactly how your working associates feel about you. This is particularly true in management, where the code of courtesy in relationships is more rigidly adhered to, even with those you dislike heartily. You have undoubtedly learned from experience how much more cooperation you can get with the low-pitched approach; you fall into the habit of talking to everyone this way, and they respond in kind. As a result of this continuing process, you may associate with a peer for years without every really getting to know his personal feelings toward you. At the same time, you build the same kind of mask over your countenance, and others have equal difficulty reading you.

There are, of course, a few basic tests of friendship on the job, some of which you would rather not employ, because they mean trouble for you. For example, when you are in a hole, which of your opposite numbers will go out of their way to give you a hand, possibly with some measure of risk to themselves? Will they voluntarily assume more than their share of a group responsibility for failure, with a consequent lightening of your culpability? (Not that you would let them do this, but do they make the offer?) Or again, do they come to you with information of value to you, when it would be just as easy to remain silent, and gain an advantage over you by doing so? Do they share their little secrets of easier ways to get the work done, or administrative shortcuts they have evolved? Again, they are giving up a potential advantage over you if they do so. Have they been known to make positive statements about your ability as a manager to those who count, at times when their remarks will be heard and evaluated?

Overt, gratuitous signs of friendship like these will not come every day or from everyone. But when they do, it should be an occasion you will never forget, and you will have incurred a debt which must someday be repaid.

It is much more probable that you will start to recognize your friends among your fellows by much less measurable signs. They will be in the areas of things not done, of advantages not pursued, and of remarks not made which could have hurt. Making friends is a fine art in which few of us are exceptionally gifted. The man who can do so is always noted by those about him, yet most of us can count on the fingers of one or two hands the real friendships which have endured over the years. Maybe this is better, because friendships can place some heavy constraints upon managerial behavior. They can cloud your judgment of others. You may hesitate just a moment too long in bringing out into the open a problem of concern to the entire organization, or pass off too lightly a sloppy performance by a friend which you would not tolerate in others. Or you may dangerously overrate performance which at best should be classified as mediocre or routine. All who are not guilty of these acts can be measured immediately for their saintly robes.

Yet, in spite of this, you are correctly concerned about being able to enumerate your friends among the other supervisors at your level. We have already commented about the role of office politics in the life of an ambitious supervisor, and your friends will do their part in this activity. Whether you are among those who believe that life runs on friendships, or are classified with the less ebullient who say that personalities should be kept out of business, there are times when a gathering of your friends at your side will give you just the amount of moral support you need to follow an unpopular course, or to stick with a decision you think is right against all opposition.

If you do store in your memory bank a tabulation of your friendships, you take on some inescapable responsibilities. First, there is no occasion in your business life where you have a right to presume on those friendships. If their support is offered, all well and good; if it is not, forget your impulse to send up a flare. They will have to make their own value judgments about when to support you and when to let you go it alone. Second, you have the same duty as they to respond with indications of friendship. It will be your obligation to determine their hour of need, and to offer your support rather than to wait to be asked.

In this chapter we will outline a methodology for rating your overall peer relationships; counting your friends is but one part of this process, and perhaps one of the lesser parts, because of the inevitable introduction of emotional bias and distortion of judgment. This broad, conceptual picture is of extreme importance to your chances for promotion, because of the undeniable influence the feelings of your peers will have on the thinking of those who make the promotional decisions. Depending upon your method of selection, this picture can be of greater or lesser importance, but it is never negligible. You can be sure that an entry will be made somewhere in the general ledger of your reputation with those who work most closely with you. Reputations *are* influential in helping careers, and nobody in his right mind will needlessly jeopardize his. So, go on with your tally of those who are with you, and use it as one of the criteria of your peer evaluation, for you will be called upon to make the same sort of input for them, sooner or later. The process is cyclical and repetitive; what you draw from this blood bank you will be expected to replace for someone else's use in their time of need. Quid pro quo, anyone?

Do Others Trust You?

Unfortunately, a person can be both universally liked and universally distrusted. How much do your peers trust you? We could further complicate matters by pointing out that some devious manipulators are thoroughly trustworthy to their subordinates, but should not be met alone in the dark by their opposite numbers. We shall not concern ourselves with this involution, since our primary target is to determine whether those who work with you feel comfortable about your general probity.

People are generally less averse to showing overt trust than they are to displaying tokens of friendship. Each of us makes daily countless gestures and signs of trust to those about us. Without hesitation, we leave personal belongings, money, and letters completely unprotected in the presence of many others. Not only do we not hesitate; these actions are usually unconscious. However, when we get into the elements of oral communication, and the sharing of our thinking, we are much more selective in opening up. We become reflexive in our judgments of those with whom we share confidences. Our rationale for doing this seldom rises to our conscious minds. If we stopped to make value judgments beforehand, we would never reveal ourselves.

It would be wise for you to take a systematic look at the amount and kinds of trust in you evinced by those who work with you. Once again, you will be forced to make a series of intuitive evaluations. If the summation of these raises a question about the level of trust in which you work, the situation is indeed serious. Only two explanations could be possible: a major character flaw within you, or an equally serious failure to communicate properly with your colleagues. In either event, some immediate repair work on your relationships is mandatory. We shall make the assumption (perhaps subject to challenge by some cynics) that you could not have achieved your present position if you had a serious character flaw. Your field of concentration should then be focused on communication, with the sole objective of correcting what is obviously a grave error. It is a defensible conclusion that if most of the respondents are misreading your messages, the fault must lie with you. Something in your encoding, your transmission, or the filtering which occurs is garbling your message. Some quick work both in analysis and in change of procedure is called for to get the desired feedback.

One of the better starts toward remedial action would be to seek the counsel of one of your best friends in conducting an in-depth analysis of your communicative process. This is no time to worry about your feelings. It is imperative that you take an objective look at what is going on in your person-to-person relationships. If your friend is indeed one, he will make a serious effort to help you in this critical operation. It is also entirely possible that he is in possession of information from other associates which he has been hesitant to convey until asked to do so.

We have already made the point that your reputation might as well be equivalent to your character, so far as your success is concerned. Let us now reinforce that concept: You have the complete trust of your associates as the result of what they *see,* rather than of what you may be. The cognitive learning necessary for survival in today's world is so immense that its total weight can play some weird tricks with your judgment, and therefore with your behavior. Sometimes your little black box rebels and starts to malfunction because of the sheer weight of the inputs it is required to process. This does not mean that you are suffering from either emotional or mental disturbance. It is merely a clogging effect from an overload of data not always relevant.

This segment of your look at your peer relationships can be a source of deep trauma unless you approach it with every vestige of objectivity you can muster. Once more, you should resist violently the impulse to panic. Human as that may be, it would be fatal to a valid analysis of your trust quotient among your peers. You must keep constantly before you how much value your fellow employees place on the matter of trust in their daily operations. In fact, their entire business life comes to a grinding halt if any significant number of their comrades are deemed to be untrustworthy. They consider themselves to be essentially honest; they have every right to demand the same from those with whom they work.

In all probability, we have blown up this matter out of proportion. The chances are very good that your analysis will result in a workable summation. The reason for emphasis on this exercise is simply that you cannot make a reasonable estimate of your relationship with your peers unless you assess their trust in you. It is necessary for balance in the composition of the total picture.

It would not be at all out of place for you to devise and use some direct testing of the extent of your associates' trust in you. This is not hard to do, nor should your attempt be too obvious. As we said, we operate so completely on a lubrication of trust that we can spot-check its presence or absence without being too conspicuous. That is, we can do this at fairly lengthy intervals. If we try to make it routine, everyone concerned gets irritated. Their reaction will be: "What goes on here? Don't you trust me?"

This situation can only result in a stalemate extremely unsatisfactory to everybody. Far better to run the check, and then proceed with business as usual until, somewhere downstream, your sensitivity alerts you to the desirability of going through the process again. It is highly unlikely that you will find the situation much changed on the second go-round, but you should be aware of personnel *and* personal changes.

Can You Give, and Receive, Cooperation?

Modern business and industry run on the wheels of cooperation. The whole job is a team effort, and we are judged by our ability to work well with others. So, one of the major facets of your peer relationships is the extent to which you can both get and give this cooperation. There are elements of a fine art involved in being able to cooperate to just the right degree for both parties concerned. It is just as bad to overcooperate as it is to fail to offer any cooperation at all. In either event, you are compromising your best work performance, and settling for less than what you need and want. To cooperate means to give some extra effort in order to help another person accomplish his objectives. The amount of energy you expend in this endeavor must be counted as a drain against the total you have available; you have an overriding responsibility to conserve your strength so that you will not ultimately fail to meet your organization's goals.

You can set some guidelines to enable you to determine the feasibility of giving your own cooperation to others. First, and inescapable, is this question: Will what you do to help your opposite number make an appreciable contribution to the whole? Second, will the expenditure of this work in any way militate against the arrival at *your* target on time? Third, how will your people react if they see that they are involved in extra work without extra remuneration? Fourth, what reaction can you expect from your supervisor if and when he learns of the transaction? The answers to all these questions are important, but do not forget, you will be required to make the final decision, and if you decide to go against the summation of the answers to these points, do so, but don't look back.

You must also consider the mirror images to these inquiries whenever you ask for another man's cooperation. He must make the same decisions, and on much the same basis. The understanding is, of course, that you will not ask for cooperation for purely selfish motives. To do so would make you vulnerable to criticism from too many people to live with the action. This is not to say that you will ever forget the ego needs which are satisfied when someone approaches you for help. It is nice to be recognized; you will enjoy knowing that another supervisor acknowledges that you can be of service to him. There are indeed times when you may decide to give cooperation purely for the good it does your psyche—if you can afford the luxury. Once more, this is your decision alone to make.

One of the mechanics of the exercise is timing. Your sensitivity will tell you when it is inadvisable to go asking for help; the work of all supervisors is similar enough to give you this feeling. Just as you would instinctively react negatively at certain times if asked to double your load, so will your peers.

We would be remiss not to look back at the remarks

we made about your friendships. This is the Achilles heel of your situation as a supervisor. Your friends will expect, consciously or not, to get a little something extra in your treatment of them. They will be hurt if you don't go out of your way to give them a lift, but you will be making a serious error if you let sentimentality influence your best judgment in these situations. Your friends have no right to make extra demands on your time and energy, any more than you have the right to do that to them. In the long run, you will be better off to say "No" than to complicate matters.

As a supervisor, you should not miss the chance to make these cooperative activities a learning experience for your people. You are responsible for their personal growth and development, and this situation can be a real stimulus. Moreover, if you play your cards right, you can develop these cooperative ventures into a participative exercise which will open their eyes to the synergy of the group, and what it can mean to the membership, individually and collectively. One result of this growth process will be an increased group cohesiveness, with an obvious intensification of observations about the achievement not only of your goals, but of those of the entire enterprise.

By achieving a reputation for good (but selective) cooperation, you will add significantly to your aura as a very good supervisor. You will burnish your image as a human being, interested in the welfare of others as well as your own. This can never hurt.

Make a place for this aspect of your peer relationships, but remember the fact that this is only one aspect of general supervisory performance. For the most part, you will still have to rely on your own efforts, and your own assets.

In the industrial jungle, the final results will be tabulated on your abilities and your efforts. You can never count on the contributions of others for more than a fraction of the total. This is as it should be. What would be the rewards if you were to be elevated and transported on the strong backs of others? The laurel wreath would be withered before you ever put it on, unless your work were the source of the award. This is what separates the men from the boys, and is why you were attracted to management in the first place. Who wants to win a fixed race?

Can You Name Your Enemies Among Your Peers?

Having stressed the importance and usefulness of your friendships among your peers, we must now consider whether any of your associates dislike you. You would be unrealistic to fail to recognize their hostility. For various reasons, most of us are more careful to conceal our feelings toward those we dislike than toward those we like. There is always the chance than an acknowledged enemy may respond with open hostility, and that he may be stronger than we are. For this reason, it is normal to avoid people we dislike, and to seek to exclude them from our circle of common contacts. So the first flare to send up in trying to discover the identity of your enemies is to list any peers in your group who conspicuously avoid you. This may be coincidental, but probably will not be.

We must make a fine distinction here. It is quite possible to have repeated confrontations with men of goodwill, if your standards are significantly different. You can have many fights with your friends without in any way endangering those friendships, so long as you stick purely to matters of principle, and sedulously stay away from personalities. Conversely, it is possible to exist in apparent peace for long periods of time beside those who cordially dislike you. Both parties may be actively avoiding the precipitation of a situation which might get out of hand. Some people even go so far as to let standards be bent rather than get into open conflict with a known enemy. This settles nothing, and at best only postpones a showdown which will have to come sometime. Perhaps it is just that you want to determine the time and place for hostilities that are likely to produce definitive results.

The personalities of your enemies will determine the manner in which they will finally show their real feelings. Overt attacks by one manager upon another are much less frequent than are more circuitous attempts on position. More bodies in the managerial arena are found with stabs in the back than with frontal wounds. Since you are adult and mature, you must be prepared for these events more or less routinely. Your enemies will make every effort to take you by surprise when they do attack, and you must be in a posture which will minimize the surprise.

Many of us consistently make a major blunder whenever we become involved in open hostility. We ignore our enemies, rather than trying extra hard to learn everything there is to know about them. You should not make this critical blunder. The more you know about your enemies, the better chance you will have of coming out on top. Your goal should be accurate prediction of their typical response to any conceivable situation. You could profit greatly from spending a reasonable amount of time in cultivating chess as a hobby. The tactical and strategic knowledge to be gained from a mastery of the game could stand you in good stead in your business life.

Do not be too impatient to spend a little time in gathering what might seem to be trivial information about your enemies. You have no way of knowing when one of these apparently minor details will take on major significance. For example, in an open battle in a staff meeting, one of the warriors emerged clearly the victor because he was aware of his opponent's habit of rearranging paper and pencils on the table before making a major point. By consistently beating him to the gun in speaking, he reduced his enemy to brooding, frustrated impotence. It was no contest. Naturally, in your quest for information about your enemies, you should be especially watchful for their blind spots and weaknesses. The cynical quip, "Never give a sucker an even break," has special meaning in managerial infighting. The exhibition of a weakness by your enemy during the action is equivalent to dropping his guard in the ring when he has a glass jaw.

Naturally you will be under the same scrutiny by your enemies. They, too, will be looking for signs of weakness and for ways to capitalize upon them. If we can make any generalization about warfare between managers, it would be that continuing advantage will be on the side of the aggressor. The necessity for defense robs us almost entirely of our discretionary movement. Very few battles have been won from a defensive position.

From the standpoint of procedure, be sure that your notes are clean and complete. Of course, this does not mean that you will commit to writing any significant amount of the data you collect. This kind of information is safe only when stored mentally. Your enemies would be delighted to stumble upon a formal record you have been amassing about them. Since this operation is in the area of security needs, your action must be basic and completely controlled by considerations of safety to yourself. The gist of this discussion revolves about the fact that you can be lulled into a dangerous position by your knowledge that effectiveness in the modern world is a measure of your success at group living.* This does not alter the fundamental truism that each is responsible for his own safety. You cannot logically expect any other person to be deeply concerned about what happens to you. They have enough to do to watch out for themselves. Yet, your progress will come from successful interactions with other people; your essential safety and self-preservation depend on your unilateral actions. This differentiation is difficult for some people to make. They are the born losers we hear so much about and see only too often.

How Do You Feel About Your Enemies?

It may be true that we react to others as they react to us, but it would be an oversimplification to say that we hate each of our enemies with exactly the same fervor they display. In the first place, as we have noted, it is entirely possible to discover with a shock that someone is an enemy whom you had considered to be at the worst neutral in his feelings about you. However, a revulsion of emotion may take place after the discovery, with a resultant reversal of your attitude toward your associate. Many strong friend-

---

*See E. T. Reeves, *The Dynamics of Group Behavior,* AMA, 1970.

ships have changed into equally strong enmities as the result of a serious quarrel, or the betrayal of one by the other over a trivial incident.

Aside from this sort of about-face, there are other considerations we should examine. If you are man enough to do it, you can gain a strong advantage over your enemy by controlling your feelings toward him, and not allowing yourself to be swayed by emotionalism where he is concerned. The man—especially the manager—who acts under the stimulus of emotion is unnecessarily handicapping himself. His reaction time will be slower; his observations will be less acute; his bias will inevitably lead him into an error of greater or lesser seriousness. Despite the principles of pure Christianity, we should not go so far as to be adamant about loving those who hate us. The point we are reinforcing here is the advantage you have if you do not allow yourself the luxury of hate, which can act as a toxin if allowed to go unchecked. Constant and unremitting stimulation of the adrenal glands can be harmful to the human body. The practice of self-control is a significant factor in your longevity.

The actions of both you and your enemy will be observed and commented on by those around you. If you maintain self-control, your reputation among your fellows will be greatly enhanced. You immediately assume the position of the man who is picked on, and Americans are well known for having sympathy for the underdog. In the eyes of your peers, you will be more the manager than your enemy. An even stronger reaction of this kind will be generated among your people when they see what is going on. Almost all people respond protectively when they see their boss attacked, even if they hadn't previously held him in too high regard. This is a devious, but observable, facet of group dynamics which has been noted hundreds of times by psychologists. It is akin to siblings who fight among themselves, but weld into a tight group the moment one member is subject to attack from an outsider.

We have mentioned before the prevalence of the art of dissembling your real feelings among the ranks of management. Too much can be lost and too little gained by displaying the depths of your emotional involvement to the casual observer. We are not suggesting that you should become a frozen-faced death mask; however, you will find it to your advantage to become slightly impassive of countenance. This appearance will, by contrast, add even more value to your smile when you do wear it.

We are, of course, speaking of one of the more complex independent variables of the human being. Interactions among people have an electrochemical basis; the complexity of the possible effects on both body and mind is hard to comprehend. Moreover, this is a reversible lane on the road of life. As your physical condition changes from day to day, so will your atttudes toward and thoughts about others. A change in the acidity of the blood hardly measurable by chemical means can entirely change your personality, as reflected in your interactions in the group. Once more, we are reminded of the necessity of developing and maintaining an iron self-discipline.

You will be spending the rest of your working life in this or another group of peers. Your living conditions on the job will be determined by the tenor of your relationships with them. If they tend to be generally healthy and pleasant, so will the climate in which you work; if they are soured, tense, and uptight, so shall you be as an individual. Although you as a person will make your mark on that group, you will also in a large measure be what your group makes of you.

This is a fine element of the supervisor's job to study in another supervisor. You undoubtedly have a hero among your associates in the matter of peer relationships. Take a deep look at his method of operation. By what means has he learned to control his indications of his personal feelings? Can you estimate closely what he thinks of any given peer of his, and if not, why not? Is he calmly impervious to the obvious enmity of one or several other supervisors? How does he act in their presence? More important, what is his attitude about them when they are absent from his immediate surroundings? The answers to some of these key questions can be invaluable to you in planning and carrying out your own day-to-day life in management circles. If your relationship with this peer is close, don't hesitate to consult with him on this problem about people. Remember, it is the problems about people which give you job security; if there were only problems about things in industry, you would soon be back on the line with your machine and its less complex enigmas. The fact that these truths are obvious does not make them any less important.

To recapitulate: The fact that you will have enemies should cause you no personal trauma, since it merely makes you a member of the largest club on earth. The way you approach your enemies, and the control you have over your responses to their hostility, will separate you from the boys. The maintenance of rigid discipline is a must; control is the password of the day.

Do You Know Your Peers off the Job?

For balance, you should know more about your peers than what you see on the job. Most people exhibit quite different traits away from work. The absence of pressure, a chance to relax, and interactions with others of your choice produce a situation where you can get to know people quickly and well. Not that you should limit your socializing to those with whom you work, for this would be narrowing and stultifying to your development; however, a judicious mixture of your colleagues into your social groups can add significantly to what you know about them. All other things being equal, this activity will also enlarge your circle of friends; ordinarily, we tend to become more friendly with the people we see often in a social context.

There are many ways in which this purpose can be accomplished unobtrusively. Golf foursomes, bowling teams, bridge groups, supper clubs, to name a few, can give you access to socialization both with other managers and with their wives and families. The latter can be an eye-opener. A little knowledge of the members of a man's family can make many of his actions more understandable. If your approach is conservative and cautious, you may be able to include a few managers at higher levels as well. The point here is to avoid at all costs the appearance of being a social climber. This facet is largely controlled by the manner of interactions of the wives concerned. If they form real friendships within the group, much value can accrue from the socializing. This comment does not mean to imply that you would expect special favor or consideration on the job as a result, but merely that at least the climate will be warm and positive.

HOW ARE YOUR PEER RELATIONSHIPS?

Another kind of off-the-job contact can be equally important: the contacts you make through memberships in service clubs or community organizations which are not purely social in purpose. We have already mentioned that it is to your benefit to build an image of interest and activity in community life. Your management is concerned with the breadth and depth of your perspective, and in how far it extends beyond the confines of the job. In these times, you can make an extremely important contribution by developing a continuing interest in and by giving service to the public schools. Since communication with our youngsters seems to be more difficult every year, our duty would lead us to do something to combat this problem. Some of the bad influences now operating within our schools can be fought effectively only by the close contact and repeated presence of many parents in school activities. A term on the school board would give you a chance for service, and would add immensely to your understanding of the modern social scene. Then, as you get new young people in your work force, you will not be completely frustrated by a total inability to communicate with them. There will also be a better chance for you to make quick progress in helping them develop the motivation they need to become good and productive members of your work group.

Getting to know your peers off the job is less important than close observation of them at work, but a combination of the two is unbeatable.

* * *

The general tone of your peer relationships will have a strong influence on your promotability. It is important that you know specifically how each of your associates thinks about you. You must know how many of them feel active friendship for you. The matter of how much they trust you is of overriding importance. Obviously, if you were unfortunately forced to make a choice between the friendship or the trust of your opposite numbers, you would have to opt for their trust. Without that, you cannot operate at all. The same can be said for the kind of cooperation you can give to others and elicit from them. The whole industrial world stands or falls on the quality of its cooperation.

The status you enjoy among your associates will be scrutinized by those responsible for picking members of middle management. The respect of the majority of your peers is a heavy plus in the ledger kept on your activities. If it is important that you be able to count your friends, it is even more so that you be able to enumerate your enemies. Hopefully, you must avoid a surprise attack from an unknown enemy, with the resultant panic that is nearly inevitable. At the same time, if possible, you should refrain from developing feelings of enmity toward them. If you can do this, your position is much stronger.

Finally, you should make a serious effort to know your peers off the job. This will complete the details necessary for your total understanding of those with whom you are working.

9

How Do You Rate Your Leadership Style?

For years management people have made the specious statement, "You must always treat all your people the same." Another dictum which has caused a great deal of misunderstanding says that "A manager must always be predictable."

Both statements belong to that huge class of delusive generalizations which father large families of fuzzy thoughts. Why should you treat all your people the same way on the job, when you do not treat all your children the same? People are individuals at work just as much as they are off the job. They have different capabilities, potential, working methods, and motivation; above all, they have different personalities. Each of these factors must be taken into consideration in your interactions with your people. Some are happiest, and do their best work, under the firm guidance of an authoritarian leader. They feel threatened when forced to make major decisions for themselves; they are much happier when they can turn to a father figure on the job to do their necessary thinking. At the opposite end of the spectrum are a few rugged individualists who resent any overt direction. They operate best under the loosest sort of guidance and leadership—all they want to know is the general boundaries of their responsibility and work assignment. These men, when properly stimulated, make fine participative subordinates. They can be prolific in generating ideas, methods, and time- and money-saving shortcuts.

Certainly, no thinking manager would approach these two extremes with the same leadership style. You would vary your methods to fit the personalities. Of course, the great majority of employees will lie between these two extremes, and they must be led in yet another manner.

Are You Locked in on a Position?

The matter of supervisory predictability lies in much the same ball park as the approach and leadership styles you use. It would be technically correct to say that it is nice (and comfortable) when the response of the leader can be predicted accurately for a given set of circumstances. But remember that you, the supervisor, will *not* have identical circumstances for any two consecutive periods of five minutes during any given day. Your reactions to these changes in your surroundings should be as fluid as the climate itself. Your people will like you better, and respect you more, if they see you consistently adapting yourself to changes as they occur.

There are, of course, times when intervening variables or crisis situations will make it mandatory that you treat the group as if it were an individual. Perhaps a sudden downturn in the economy has had severe repercussions in your business, and things are quite grim. If you have been working in a generally permissive atmosphere in order to encourage participation and creativity, common sense would dictate a tightening of the reins, and perhaps even a flick of the whip. This is the quickest way (and the only sure one) to make all your people recognize the seriousness of your predicament. When they understand this, they will be happy to have you run a tight ship until the emergency has passed. In fact, they will have more confidence in you for having done your job to protect the positions of the entire crew.

The possibility of locking yourself into one leadership style is a real and present danger. You find early in your management career a method of approach with which you feel comfortable, and which seems to be functional for a variety of situations. Before you know it, you have habituated yourself to its use, and do not think of the necessity of being ready to change. Then, when major changes occur in your environment, you find yourself mysteriously ineffective as a leader. This naturally puts you under tension, and the vicious circle is enlarged as you become more and more ineffective because of your own pressures. It is a short step from this position to the panic button and complete loss of control of your working unit. In the long run, it is much safer and productive of higher overall quality of leadership to recognize the necessity for changing your style to accommodate to situations as they really are. The modern leader has in his group people of unparalleled sophistication and awareness. They are a great deal more critical of their leadership than were their fathers or grandfathers. Actually, for most members of the new work force, there is no such thing as situational respect for the nominal leader. He must earn whatever status is accorded to him by his group, and that status will be subject to day-by-day scrutiny and review. Your crown of leadership has no anchor on your head.

One corollary of this principle should not pass without observation. In preparing for your desired promotion, you should not forget that the middle manager finds himself under the necessity of making compromises much more often than he did in his previous position. The pressures to which he is subjected, and which come at him from above, from his peers, and from his subordinates, can be equalized or neutralized most of the time only by tradeoffs. You have undoubtedly contributed enough pressure to your boss's life to understand this point. In fact, if you are a normally adept operator, you have engineered situations which forced your superior to give you a desired objective as a compromise with your originally stated position. He knows this as well as you do, and will respect you for looking after your own interests in an acceptable fashion. He would have severe doubts about your promotability unless he knew you were capable of using this ploy when it is clearly indicated. The point to remember is that you must be infinitely flexible in your approach to the leadership of the people under your direction. The best crews are those led by managers who can vary their leadership styles.

Is There Mutual Trust and Confidence with Your People?

We have spoken of the importance of having the trust of your peers. If there had to be a choice, however, it would be much more important that you have the trust and confidence of your people than that of your peers. No manager can do his work without this kind of relationship with his subordinates. As a manager, much of what you do has proprietary value either for the corporation at large or for your part of it. You could not begin to keep the records for your area unless you had implicit faith in your secretary and several clerks. Needless to say, you would not be able to do all the record keeping yourself. Ordinarily, wage and salary information for the management group is classified top secret, yet several of the general office people—again, clerks and secretaries—know much of this secret information. And they have to trust you completely, or you could not administer a salary program within your group. The same can be said for manufacturing processes, quality-control tests, price quotations from vendors, the mass of records generated by labor relations, and so forth.

Since you are only one person, you cannot possibly keep a minute-by-minute check on the whereabouts and actions of all the people reporting to you. You trust them. You have faith in their desire and ability to keep themselves productively occupied at the tasks of the group for most of the working day. This is true even if your attitude is basically negative, since no man can simultaneously and continuously monitor all of his work area. Your future resides in the job activities of your people, and you put your trust in their probity every day.

By the same token, your employees individually put trust in their personal future completely in your hands. By remaining with you over an extended period of time, they are reinforcing their confidence in you as a leader. In a sense, their trust in you is the greater, since they tie both their future and that of their family to you as an individual, while your trust is with the group. You have the advantage of being able to survive the defection of one or two members of your crew, but if you fail them, many people will be victimized. Yet it is obvious that the two-way flow of trust is necessary for the viability of any business organization.

Although the matter of mutual trust and confidence is almost never formalized or put into writing, its presence or absence is easily discernible to an inexperienced observer, and your public image is greatly shaped and influenced by it.

You might say, completely sincerely, that the trust of your people will be strongly correlated with your predictability. Therefore, you could be forgiven if at first you decided to freeze into one managerial style and refuse to budge from it. No matter how logical this approach might seem, it is fallacious. Your people's complete trust *must* be based at least partly on their belief in the cogency of your thinking. They would be the first to admit, if they speak honestly, that you can be unpredictable and still be worthy of their confidence. They will trust you if they have faith in your ability to analyze your people and approach them in the manner you decide is consonant with their individual character and mode of response to a stimulus.

The greatest threat to losing the faith of your people lies in faulty communication. Literally thousands of volumes have been written, and millions of words spoken, on the necessity for good modes and methods of communication, and for ways of evaluating communications. But it is still worthy of your careful attention and thought that one botched major job of communicating can irreparably damage the trust your people have in you.

Perhaps the hairier aspect of this problem is the possibility of your failure to communicate a critical item. Subordinates have a way of looking at this failure as outright treachery. They are as interested as you are in any events which affect them, and you know how angry you become when you are left out of the normal communications loops. You are subject to the same unreasoning anger against the culprit as they are, and for the same reasons.

Maintaining the flower of trust is relatively simple, although it is a tender bloom. Tend the communications channels, keep the data flow regular and normal, actively solicit feedback and critiques, and you should have no problems in keeping your relationships clean and productive. For your own sake, you should occasionally run an audit of the trust you enjoy from your people. Essentially, it doesn't matter if they know you are doing so. If your relationships are right, they will respond positively, as another indication that they respect you as a leader and are continuing to cast their lot with yours.

When this kind of atmosphere pervades your organization, it is tremendously supportive to eliciting trust from others. All of us are sensitive to what a leader's people think of him; unless he has a gross and obvious character flaw, the trust of his people is a large sum of money in the bank for him to draw on in his other corporate relationships. For this reason, a major effort on your part is called for to promote this climate beyond the confines of your own group. The more sections of the organization which can be organized into a network of trust, the greater the results which can be expected in all positive aspects of the enterprise's activities. From a personal standpoint, positive evidences of this activity will be a big plus in your management's judgment of your leadership and general ability as a manager. Casting your bread upon the waters has more uses than development of the biceps and the attraction of waterfowl.

How Sensitive Are You to Your Impact on Subordinates?

Each of us has a self-image which allows us to be comfortable in our surroundings most of the time. We adjust to others with a variety of reactions according to the personality of the individual with whom we have contact at the moment; thus, the same action toward us by two people can produce two widely different reactions in us.

Because of your position of leadership in your crew, your personality has an intensified impact on each of your subordinates. You are the boss; your actions carry heavier weight simply from that fact. It may never have occurred to you that an action you performed in goodwill could cause anything but a positive reaction by your subordinates. Nothing could be further from the truth. There might be a wide range of reactions from your people, varying from the strongly positive to the violently negative. Because of this, by far the better course would be for you to assume deliberately a management style calculated to elicit a particular response from your contact of the moment on the basis of your knowledge of him. You are not concerned in the long run with what he thinks of your personality, but you are deeply involved in what he will do as a result of your giving orders, counseling, or other supervisory contact. It is even conceivable that under certain exigencies you might decide you wanted your approach to anger an employee, if you thought that would stimulate him to abandon an apathetic attitude. With someone else, you would use a more conciliatory approach of pure reason, basing your hopes on an intellectual reaction from him. In the same situation, you might decide to joke with a third person, and keep a light tone to the encounter.

When you are in contact with your entire group, your management style would be based on your analysis of the group personality. Here you would be strongly influenced by the informal leadership style and by your prediction of the way your group would react. If you want to pursue a devious course, and you are at odds with informal leadership, set up the situation so that you are urging them to do the opposite of your real desires, and then let the informal leaders sway the group to behave as you wanted them to in the first place.

Group efficiency and effectiveness are strongly affected by the style of the manager. If you have taken into account the salient intervening variables, and know intimately the makeup of your people, you have an excellent chance to play some pretty tunes by careful choice of different managerial styles under differing internal conditions.

The prime target is to increase your sensitivity to the reaction of others to your style of the moment. In these cases, you will never be able to depend on verbal feedback, since none will be given except under the provocation of deep emotional disturbance. What they say is ordinarily of far lesser import than what they are doing at the moment. The nonverbal cues will be there for you to read loud and clear as soon as you condition yourself to be aware of them. Facial expressions, body stances, movements of hands or feet, eye movements, contact or lack of contact through the eyes, doodling, shuffling of papers, foot tapping, and a hundred other signs—each can tell you something about the reception and interpretation of your message to your people. Once more we should reinforce that these are personal responses from differing personalities. It is your job to get to know your people so that you can properly interpret what they are sending in the way of feedback to your signal.

Are You Aware of Your Own Anxiety?

You should be on the lookout for one result not ordinarily predictable. As you get closer to a knowledge of your readiness for promotion to middle management, your own anxiety level will rise rapidly. There will be an inevitable effect on your personality, temporary though it may be. You can expect yourself to be a little sharper and more brusque than usual, and this will of course evoke a reaction from your people. They will be surprised and disturbed—even angry—to have you apparently criticizing them for something which before would not have aroused you. If they respond with irritation or pique, you in turn may escalate your atypical response. And so it goes. It would be hard to overemphasize the sensitiveness of interpersonal reactions at this stage in your development. More than one promising candidate for the really important promotion has been scuttled by unfortunate reactions to his own hypersensitivity.

Concomitant with the cultivation of awareness of your impact on others is the necessity for extra-rigid self-control during these trying times. You cannot afford to let yourself go in the same way you could have a few years ago when you were still on the line. It is entirely acceptable for a line worker to vent his spleen on his surroundings with impunity; the manager, because of his position, is subject to the rigors of noblesse oblige. This is the time for the introduction of calculated bits of R & R—rest and rehabilitation, as it is known in the military. You are just as subject to combat fatigue as is the front-line soldier in wartime, but you will not be as easily forgiven for aberrant behavior as will he. You will find it helpful to keep constantly in mind the complexity of the relationships in your group, of which you are the hub and the communications center. Everything of any importance is channeled through you; if it is not, you are in big trouble, and you can forget about any promotion.

Be aware; be alert; be reactive; be adaptable; be ready for the unexpected. These are the watchwords of these particular days of your development. This is the second great crisis in your career, and only a little less important than was your promotion to supervision.

Do Your Peers Think You Are a Leader?

We have already indicated a concern about whether your associates like you, dislike you, or are neutral toward you. But there is another consideration of much more importance to your advancement: Do your peers have respect for your leadership ability, even to the point of turning to you to guide them in times of stress? Management expects its candidates for middle management to be leaders of leaders, and to demonstrate this ability indisputably before promotion is solidified.

Several kinds of leadership exist. The informal group recognizes this fact by practicing rotational leadership: They pass the baton to one person for emergency leadership, to another for planning strategy, to still another for social activities, and so on. As nearly as is possible, the middle manager must show strength in several kinds of leadership. This capacity must be clearly evident to a majority of those who know him, up to the point of their being willing to let him lead them in many different situations.

Lest there be misunderstanding, it should be pointed out that political leadership does not always carry great weight with the executive level. It may or may not help your career to have been an officer in your management club, or in the local Jaycees. If ability in politics and vote getting is your only sign of leadership, it will make little impression on most managers, and might do you harm in their estimation. Whether the judgment is valid or not, large numbers of executives actually mistrust politicians, and tend to limit their business with them. But your management will be deeply interested if they see your fellow supervisors turning to you for counsel in their day-to-day business activities, and especially so if you have influence beyond your own department. When those in other functions or disciplines turn to you for leadership, it is highly significant.

This is one phenomenon you can do little on your own to either generate or increase. The recognition will come spontaneously or not at all. No one has ever discovered a way to create leadership by either influence or legislation. The potential booby trap here is obvious: Once established, the pattern of seeking you out for leadership can make you (if you are less than completely mature) come to think of yourself as the universal authority, and this is a powerful boomerang. This self-image is a professional hazard among doctors and engineers, because of the high incidence of sycophancy among their immediate associates. If you find yourself showing signs of increasing leadership among your fellow supervisors, examine yourself ruthlessly at frequent intervals for any indication of this malignant illness.

There is little correlation between chronological age and the appearance of leadership qualities. Many extremely young people emerge as powerful leaders among their fellows, although such ability usually develops with a little maturity in years.

Overt acknowledgment of leadership in another person is rare. We ordinarily show it in our actions, rather than in open communication. Do you consistently have lunch with your own group, or with someone else's? Do others come spontaneously to your work area or office to talk with you, or do you do most of the traveling? Do you have an influence on the dress and hobbies of your group, or do you follow the signals given by others?

There is great meaning also in the people to whom you turn for your leadership. If your supervisory group is large, it is probable that several members will show good leadership qualities. Who among them do you respect enough to turn to when you need guidance and counseling? Or do you ordinarily go a rung or two higher in the organization to find your mentor?

It is highly probable that you will find yourself instinctively varying the managerial styles you use with those who seek your leadership from outside your group. This is one of the reasons why they seek you out. It will be obvious to you that these are individuals, and therefore are vastly different in both their needs for and their response to leadership.

As this leadership of peers emerges, it will cause a change in your levels of influence in the organization. You will now be listened to respectfully by those in higher levels of management. You may come to have a hand in the development of policy in your own and other departments long before you are at the nominal policy-making level. This is good, since it will give you practice in one of the most elemental executive skills, should your ambition lead you to zero in on that level as an eventual target.

You must be careful that these new activities do not steal too much time and thought from your regular job. You cannot afford for one moment either in actuality or in appearance to be neglecting your work, since it is, after all, the one and finally most important criterion by which you will be promoted, or fail in the effort.

To recapitulate: You must carry on your present job under a full head of steam, and still be prepared to cope with the problems and challenges of your newly developed leadership among your peers. This is another of the innumerable tests you must meet and pass before you are knighted and allowed to assume the richer cloak.

If you have noted that life is becoming increasingly complicated, your perception is to be commended. There is little likelihood that the tempo will slacken in the foreseeable future.

How Do You React to a Changing Work Force?

As mentioned before, it is a human trait to want predictability in leadership. The same desire operates in most leaders. They want to be able to forecast with some degree of reliability how their people will react under given circumstances. That is becoming more difficult because of the different values, motivations, life styles, and behavior patterns of some of the workers now entering employment for the first time. The leader finds it increasingly hard to decide what managerial style to use as these new people come under his supervision; he is forced to guess more than he likes, and a correct guess in one instance does not mean that the same style would work the second time around.

Increasing changes are also occurring in the older members of work groups as they come under the influence of some of these new social influences. Few events can disturb a manager more than to have an old faithful employee suddenly display atypical behavior and apparently lose sight of the major goals of the enterprise. How do you play this one? Do you assume that the aberrant actions will be short-lived, and do nothing? Do you start on an intensive program of ferreting out the causes of this change, and run the risk of alienating an old friend? Do you formalize the whole matter by giving him a special performance review, so that you can put in black and white the undesirable alterations you see in his actions? These are not easy questions for you, the supervisor, to face. You have much to lose if these negative elements become permanent; yet you can hardly stand by and do nothing when a good employee seems to be going to pot before your eyes.

From your supervisory standpoint, many group effects will be observable from the admixture of these different new employees. One of the first symptoms of malaise will be a lessening of your group's cohesiveness. Splinter groups will coalesce around some of the more articulate people; in many cases, their informal leadership will be strong. There will be some sharp and pointed questioning of your objectives, and you will find it necessary to defend your goals again and again to people who never questioned them before. Your own anxiety level is likely to rise significantly. Conflict in the group will almost certainly ensue, because the older members feel that the smooth operation they have been used to is now threatened. Your leadership is going to be tested as it never has been since you first became a supervisor, and you will have to work much harder than you had expected to achieve your objectives.

Your duty will be onerous but clear: You need to take on these people one by one and get them into line as functional members of your group, or separate them. Distasteful though it may be to you, a time of 9.1 managerial style may lie ahead of you, not only with the newcomers but with the entire group, until you are sure that the major threat to your operational efficiency has been eliminated and that the dissenters have been properly inducted and absorbed as regular members of your crew. This is only another example of the fact that today's supervisor is primarily a manager of change, and that the only certainty in your working life as a supervisor from here on out will be the appearance of change and the necessity of working it into your scheme of things without precipitating a major crisis or losing your operational competence. The one hope in sight is that you will probably have the wholehearted cooperation of your older crew members when they see what your task is and how you are approaching it. They will be with you all the way, for self-protection.

Man's essential nature has not changed; however, with an increasingly complex society evolving about us, man *does* vary his behavior experimentally, and he either runs and hides or stands and fights as he perceives threats to his survival. All these variables will go into the mix of the reactions of your crew members to what they see going on around them. It is not necessary for the forces to exist on the job; they will bring their hyperactivity to the business scene if they are disturbed by events outside their working environment.

You are yourself not immune, of course, to the same

new factors, and you will have to exercise self-control to a degree never before required in order to retain your composure and to do the job with your employees.

One of the better moves for you and your people is to seek out the right kind of training (or retraining) methods, and proceed at once with activity designed to lessen the tensions and to divert some of the extra adrenaline so that it will flow into constructive channels. Apprehensions will be lowered in two ways: by getting to know the face of the stranger (the projected change), and by taking action. However, keep in mind that this is only a therapeutic measure, and you cannot afford to lose sight of the main objectives you have set for yourself and your group. This would be self-defeating.

You are not required to carry this load without help. Your supervisor must know what is going on, and you have the resources of all the other managers in the enterprise at your call. Also remember that they are undergoing the same experience, and some of them have developed methods of meeting these changing conditions which you will find useful.

Can You Grow as a Leader?

We have been somewhat preoccupied with an examination of your present status, and with methods for helping you to develop yourself. There is another question of much more urgent importance than anything discussed so far: How much potential do you have left for further growth as a leader? If you move into middle management, you will be directly supervising fewer people than you now do, but there are some major differences in the leadership you will be required to show.

In the first place, you will be supervising other managers. We have already examined part of this arrangement, but have not yet emphasized how important the depth and quality of your leadership will be to the success of your organization. Remember, you will be receiving, interpreting, and transmitting downward all new essential company policies. This means you must be able to evoke the fullest cooperation and support from your subordinate supervisors. There must be no doubt about your commitment, and theirs, to the implementation of every directive from the executive level. Once established and signed off, there can be no further hesitation. In many cases, this will be a test of the quality of your leadership, since new policy is notorious for inciting resistance, if for no other reason than that it is new and represents a change in the status quo. You can personalize this by recalling your own reaction at various times to new procedures, and how your supervisor handled your conversion to conformity.

The second element of the middle management job which will require a new facet to your leadership is the fact that there will almost certainly be more than one function or discipline subject to your leadership. You may have to take different approaches to the various segments of your staff in order to get their complete accord. For example, if you have personnel from both manufacturing and quality control reporting to you through separate lines, you will have to remember their quite different orientation toward the job to be done. The manufacturing people are totally centered on getting the product out the door; the quality control people are sublimely indifferent to quantity, but deeply immersed in consideration of conformity to minimal specifications of quality. Their rationale for a new directive will be very different from the one accepted by the manufacturing people. It is your job to see that both are enthusiastic in putting the new policy into practice.

Your leadership will be further tested in the area of your newly required conceptual skills. Your field of vision will have been significantly broadened, and you will find it necessary to conceptualize a much larger part of the total operation. You must then be able to translate this understanding into something relevant for your people, and make it take on meaning for them. This implies greater demands upon your capacity for empathy, for you must realize that your subordinates are still concerned only with their small part of the total picture, and will not be too sympathetic to the problems of their peers. Your part is to catalyze the reaction which will meld your group into a functioning whole.

Basically, it is in the area of leadership that you will have acquired your new status and dignity. It is for your ability as a leader that your management will have graphically increased your salary and your sphere of influence. The administrative parts of your new job are not that much greater or more demanding to warrant your change in station. In fact, you may find that you have fewer onerous administrative duties as a middle manager than you had as a first-line supervisor, since your new status will carry with it staff positions designed to relieve you of much tedious detail. You are now truly expected to delegate work in fact as well as in theory. This is the sticking point which proves fatal to many new middle managers: They try desperately to function as three or four (or more) first-line supervisors, rather than growing into their leadership responsibilities with the concomitant demands for more delegation.

In the interests of moderation, we should remind you that the change now facing you is smaller than the one you made when you entered supervision; that is, you will not now be required to make an entirely new orientation to your job. Most of the changes which will occur when you are promoted will be of degree rather than of kind. Your leadership requirements will be heavier, but they will be familiar in general context.

The one major change entailing a completely new concept will be your frequent association with the executive level. Their problems and concentration are far removed from anything in your previous work experience, and you will have to translate these experiences into your own language and understanding. Moreover, you will frequently be called upon to pass down the line relevant bits of this action to your subordinates. This buffer relationship will continue as long as you are in middle management, and will always constitute a large part of your responsibility. Just as heretofore you communicated the wishes of middle management to hourly workers and salaried personnel, you will now transmit executive communications to the first line of supervision. In the final analysis, this is a change in emphasis rather than in basic nature.

It is not realistic to expect that this growth in your leadership can actually occur before your promotion. That development is too much a product of the situation to be created artificially. In other words, there is no real way to practice being a middle manager. You will have to be tested under fire after being moved into the real situation.

Perhaps this is just as well, but you should be aware of what lies before you so that you will not be taken by surprise when the occasion arrives.

* * *

Your leadership style will take on new importance as you enter middle management, since you will now be managing other managers, who have more rigid expectations from their superiors than you have been used to up to now. The first consideration is that you not be locked in on any one managerial style, but that you be prepared to be flexible, and to change according to external situations or changes in your personnel. It is of utmost importance that you establish an easy sense of mutual trust and confidence with your people. This requirement will grow as you go up each echelon.

Right now, you should assay the impact you have on your subordinates as a person (and a personality) to be sure that abrasiveness is at a minimum. Parallel to this, you must review your rating among your peers as a leader of men. Do you have their respect in this area? At the same time, you will be vitally concerned with your ability to ride with the punches thrown at you by a rapidly changing work force.

All these factors will require you to grow as a leader as you make the move to middle management.

10

What's Your Boss Saying to You?

MOST students of management say that, although communications both up and down the line are universally bad, they are much worse going up the line than down. It would be difficult to generalize as to whether this is a discouraging attitude on the part of the superior, or whether it comes from the subordinate's reluctance to commit himself by means of uncalled-for communication. It is probably a combination of these two factors plus a third variable—oversight or plain carelessness. In any event, the man who knows how, when, and what to send up the line in the way of information will be promoted, all other things being equal. We shall assume that you learned *how* to communicate with your boss a long time ago, and shall concentrate on *what* you should tell him.

How Much Do You Tell Your Boss?

As a general principle, you would do well in this area to practice management by exception. You know well how busy your supervisor is; he will appreciate your effort to conserve his time and energy if you pass along to him only those items which are both important and exceptional. He is already deluged by a torrent of communications from many sources. The reports deemed necessary demand a significant chunk of his time. One method found successful by many supervisors is to pass the news along by means of short, crisp memos, each dealing with but a single item. You should take great care to limit your reports to the barest essentials. If your boss wants to know more, he can always ask you for the added information.

Most assuredly, you should inform your supervisor completely about any unusual money matters. This narrows down in most cases to anticipated overruns of the budget, or sudden and unexpected capital outlay items. More disturbance and unfavorable reaction will be generated by unexpected money troubles than by any other aspect of the manager's job. If the advice, "Never surprise the boss," has any validity, it is in the fiscal area. This is natural, since upper management places such a high value on the proper handling of money. A large number of company top executives are financial men; any disturbance in their sphere of influence is extremely upsetting to them.

This, of course, does not mean that you could expect never to be taken by surprise by a money emergency. What is important is that you communicate quickly and completely whenever this situation arises.

Incidentally, it should be obvious from the foregoing that in order for you to fulfill this obligation you must have created a fine channel of communications with your people. The fiscal emergency, like all others, has its roots where the action is—on the line, with the people you are currently supervising. Whether it is the replacement of defective machinery, the sudden need for unscheduled overtime, or any other situation, the urgency of getting this information to your boss cannot be overemphasized. He will thank you for alerting him.

A second category of necessary communications is often found in the materials your crew uses routinely. The exceptions occur with events such as vendor failure, errors in shipping, receipt of defective materials, and so on. Since materials are so closely allied with the manufacturing process, any disturbance in this area quickly assumes the proportions of a major crisis. Even though in most instances your superior will immediately redelegate the matter to you to handle, it is still of utmost importance that you apprise him of conditions. He would be seriously embarrassed to have the incident brought up in his boss's staff meeting, and to have to admit ignorance of the matter. The logistics of big business is, at present, one of its most critical and vulnerable areas. So much can happen between dispatching the purchase order and receiving the desired goods that it is a wonder materials ever arrive on time. If you can in any way serve as an expediter of the flow of materials for your crew, you will accrue many favorable points in your superior's book.

The third major category of needed upward communications has to do with people. Heading the list are outstandingly good and outstandingly bad performances by any of your employees. Unchallenged at the top of the heap is the absolute necessity of notifying your superior of your proposed intentions in disciplinary matters. Owing to the current involvement (either in actuality or by implication) of the federal government in areas of discipline, through the National Labor Relations Board, you must document fully and completely every action you propose to take. In most companies, final disposition of these cases rests at the third, fourth, or fifth level of management. Although you are the fulcrum of the action, you will almost never have autonomy in it; however, you will be essential in proposing dispositions of cases, since you are the one in possession of the facts, and are personally involved in the primary event.

We should not overlook the other side of the coin: the exceptionally good performance of any of your people. Remember that you first attracted the attention of your boss as a possible candidate for middle management because of your better-than-average performance on a continuing basis.

You should monitor these three general areas faithfully and continuously. Through this activity in your group, you will have an effect on the general health and well-being of your superior's job. Naturally, we are acting under another assumption—if you are a genuine candidate for promotion into middle management, your relationship with your superior will be easy and comfortable.

Most of the communications activity mentioned here will be formalized in writing, but will be amplified and strengthened by face-to-face discussions.

What Does Your Boss Tell You?

There is great polarization in the thinking about management communication down the line. Many people feel that each level has information which should be cut off there, in the interest of security. Their rationale is that proprietary information should be held within as tight a circle as possible. This is a suspect argument for many reasons. First, are not managers members of management at whatever level they occupy in the hierarchy? Why would they be more likely to violate security simply because they are one level lower down? However, it is true that danger of security leaks increases greatly every time the circle of those in the know is enlarged. Second, we must face a fundamental fact of human psychology: Each of us takes a secret small delight in possessing information not available to others. We rationalize by saying that this bit of company knowledge should be kept tight; actually, no great harm might be done if every employee in the company were aware of it.

This tendency to restrict the flow of information is one of the greatest barriers in business communication. Its opposite is the supervisor's tendency to transmit upward only those things he feels his boss would be pleased to hear. He works on the entirely fallacious assumption that he can sweep something under the rug so that his superior will never hear it. The man who can avoid both of these common booby traps is well on the way to becoming an expert communicator in business. This is one of the most critical elements which will determine whether you are promoted into middle management, or will later have an opportunity to be selected as an executive.

Meanwhile, what items can you both expect and demand your boss to tell you routinely? At the top of the list is one broad generalization: *If an item of information has any bearing on your day-to-day operations, your boss has no right to keep it from you.* Nothing is more maddening or embarrassing than to hear from a peer in another department something critical to the conducting of business in your crew. There can be no excuse for your superior to fail to get these necessary bits of information to you expeditiously. If he knows he will be absent, it is his duty to set in motion some mechanism for the transmittal of routine information. Perhaps he will designate a stand-in during his absence; maybe he will empower his secretary to pass along the news. In any event, some method of accomplishing this procedure must be established. Of course, you are currently under the same obligation to your subordinates, and they will be justifiably critical of you if you fail in this duty.

A second major category of items your boss will pass on to you are those he judges to be not critical but "nice to know." These constitute the general background knowledge which will enable you to discriminate more finely in your decisions, and will raise your performance from average to excellent. For example, your superior may have come by accident into possession of not widely known information about a competitor. By sharing it with you, he has given you that shade of advantage over your competition so valuable to your chances for promotion.

The third kind of information your superior should communicate to you freely consists of ideas, plans, philosophy, and the general nature of his thinking about everything connected with the business. He can demonstrate here the true quality of his leadership, and can contribute hugely to your development as a manager. These items can seldom be planned. They will be triggered by the situation of the moment, and, in fact, would lose much of their relevance if removed from context. The encouragement of this flow will be largely your responsibility. It is only when your superior recognizes your eagerness to receive these bits that he will be motivated to continue the process. This is, of course, a reciprocal arrangement. You will be expected to contribute your input to the conversation, if for no other reason than for the feedback involved, and to assure him that you are reading him correctly.

The average manager spends 90 percent of his working time in some form of communication. He must be highly selective in choosing his content if he is going to maintain the efficiency of his personal operation. You have no time to waste in the transmittal of trivia—unless it is for the perfectly justifiable intent of establishing rapport with another person. This will, naturally, not be necessary between you and your boss after the first few days of your association. Nor should you assume that there is no place in business or industry for personal small talk between associates. If you are both lovers of professional football, a reasonable postmortem of the weekend's games is completely justifiable on a Monday morning. This interchange will be instrumental in formulating your superior's evaluation of your personality and character. The pictures of these qualities, when derived solely from straight business activities, can be pretty sterile.

Are There Intimations of Immortality?

There is a saying in management circles that no man should ever be promised a promotion. The theory is that it should be mentioned only when a firm offer for advancement is tendered. This dictum is honored more in the breach than in the observance. A superior cannot prepare a subordinate properly for advancement without giving an occasional hint of what is in the superior's mind. That is, if the candidate did not have some idea of what was going on, he would be far too insensitive to be a prospect.

If the time and situation are about right for you to be tabbed, you will be getting more and more frequent cues of what is in the air. Many of these will come in the form of deeper probing in the area of your development program. Your boss will want to be satisfied that you have done everything possible to be ready for the next big step. If he is alert to the changes you will be undergoing, much of his concern will be about the growth of your conceptual ability. Since you have had little use for this skill as a first-line supervisor, and since it will now suddenly become a critical aspect of your job, he will be justified in wanting to know whether you have done any preparation in this area. More queries will be directed to him from higher management about this than about any other facet of your development.

Another cue that you are being considered for promotion will be the sly intimations sent to you from your superior concerning the personalities and working habits of his group of peers. Your orientation into middle management can be made much smoother and less awkward if you have at least a basic understanding of your new associates. To a lesser extent, the same thing will be done for the executive echelon to whom you will soon be reporting. Actually, since they are the big men in the company, more general information about them is widely disseminated than about middle management. You may already have a fair mental image of most of the executives. Nevertheless, your superior would be remiss not to add to your knowledge.

About now, management will show new and more penetrating interest in your community and public-service activities. If you are not participating in one of these endeavors, some strong efforts may be made to interest you in joining a service club. If your enterprise is located in a medium-size or small community and has great influence on the general public, you may be asked to think about joining a country club. In many companies, where this membership is a semiofficial business activity, your initiation fees and dues might be picked up by your employer. A lot of intercompany liaison work is done in these surroundings.

You should not necessarily assume that these things will be considered in any sense as orders. They will be more on the plane of suggestions for you to weigh and evaluate. If you feel there is an advantage either to you or to the business in making such a move, you would naturally do so. The main point is not to be stampeded into too many such moves too quickly. You will be undergoing a significant reorientation on the job, and this *must* come first. If your development has been sound, and is recognized as such by those above you, you should sense a new and greater freedom in making decisions. You will be expected to pick up a much heavier share of the load, and this will entail making more and more important judgments.

Your immediate superior will not be the only person concerned in these hints and allusions. His associates, and some of his superiors, will be in more frequent contact with you than they have been before. Efforts will be made to have these occasions seem casual and perfectly normal, but you will be able to feel the difference. This will be a difficult time for your personal feelings. No matter how confident you may feel of your eventual promotion, there is always the nagging knowledge that nothing is certain until it has been formalized. You will remember others who had seemed to be heading straight for a climb, only to have something happen to their chances, so that their plans never materialized. You are bound to become a little jumpy and nervous, but it is of great urgency that you maintain good self-control during this trying period. Overreacting now means that you are failing the last great test before the action. Counsel freely with your boss; ask his advice if you feel it necessary, but he will still insist that you make most of these decisions for yourself. Not to do so would negate all the training and preparation you have been undergoing since you entered supervision.

Above all else, be observant of these communications as they go down the line—both for the information involved, and for the purpose behind them. Review them frequently, and don't be afraid to keep notes for yourself on what is happening. This is the last briefing you will get before the coach sends you into the big game; both his reputation and yours are on the line. Remember, you do have one tremendous asset going for you: the goodwill of your superior and the people further up the line. They would not be putting you into this situation unless they had strong confidence that you can perform up to standards as a member of middle management.

To diagram all the factors which affect a promotion would be a literal impossibility. The process is too complex for any one person to visualize completely; he cannot even know all the facts germane to the action, since so many people are involved in the creation of a new member of middle management. The best you can do is to become as aware as possible of the many variables, and to maintain a climate, if not the strict actuality, of total objectivity. This is a responsibility of both the candidates and those who make the actual decision.

Does Your Boss Open the Pipeline Upward?

Your superior does not complete his communicative responsibility to you by sending things down the line to you. If your company follows normally accepted procedures, he is the kingpin in the linkage of communications between you and all echelons above him. True, in everyday business practice, you will often have casual (nearly routine) contact with the executive level without going through him. Usually, however, you will observe protocol by initiating upward messages through the office of your superior. He can expedite this activity materially. Depending upon the depth and complexity of your organizational structure, he will report either to a layer of upper middle management or to an executive. In larger businesses, it is often difficult to gain access to one of these people. If your communication is written, and intended for upper management as a final target, you can go one of two ways: You may address the memo to your boss, with carbon copies to the executives, or you may reverse that procedure. If the document is of critical importance, your man can give you a special boost by enclosing his copy with a cover memo to his superior with his comments on principal items. If, on the other hand, you have reason to communicate orally with an executive, especially if he is not in your direct line, a path-clearing phone call from your superior may open doors much more easily.

Your superior can give you another big lift by his informal talks with executives. He might casually mention a project with which you are currently occupied that is of interest to them, so that they will be receptive when you approach them with a report on it. It is easy to see that the most important help your superior can give you in upward communications is to create in the minds of top management a favorable image of you and your work. This is not done overnight, and should be begun well in advance of the timing of your proposed promotion. It will be one of your first direct experiences of the self-imposed isolation in which most executives work.

A huge percentage of executives' contacts are with their peers; they may go days or weeks without seeing more than a few of their subordinates. This widespread habit of executives is bitterly denounced by managers everywhere. Some claim that it produces a stricture in the channel of upward communications so that executives are dangerously underinformed about activities in their own company. They may know much more about the daily operations in a competitor's place of business. The only positive arguments for this isolation are that it maintains greater objectivity of judgment, and gives the executive more discretionary time for the real purpose of his job: the making of long-range decisions. In effect, your boss is elected to run interference for you against this defensive posture. This is probably the only way you can effectively get to the executives with desirable and necessary information.

A third method your boss might elect to strengthen your upward communication is to delegate you to represent him from time to time at his superior's staff meeting, or to make presentations and proposals personally to upper management. In the latter case, he will probably go with you, but put you on your own so far as the actual presentation is concerned. These two techniques are recognized as standard developmental activities for managers at any level, since they allow superiors to see the man operating in a pressure situation. This is one of the key factors used to evaluate any candidate for promotion. You will be getting much more than simple feedback to your upper communication during this kind of exercise. If you are alert, you can learn a great deal about the personalities and operating methods of the men responsible for final decisions in your company. If you are as sensitive as you should be, one or two of these experiences can give you a good line on your friends and enemies at the executive level.

So You Want to Be a Manager!

Do You Know the Executives?

These details represent another of your developmental items on which thorough records should be kept. Over the months, you should accumulate dossiers on all important members of upper management. Don't depend on your own mental ability to keep all the details active. It is wise to review a record of this sort before you have any formal contact with an executive. He is more apt to be impressed with you if you apparently have a good knowledge of him. You should *not* assume from this that you are being advised to cultivate the image of the all-American boy. By this time, you should be too mature a manager for this image to be necessary. Rather, the objective is to give the impression of a manager who knows his business, and who is aware of the importance of his contacts with any superior.

Your total image among the managers above you in the hierarchy is a highly unstable accumulation of long years of events in your daily performance, plus the record of single, and unrelated, incidents. Unfortunately, the latter may have greater weight in the minds of the observers than the former. That is, your business record will be heavily weighted by a series of critical events. They will be noted and evaluated by many managers, who will compare their impressions and opinions whenever performances are evaluated. It is frustrating to anyone to have so little control over how he looks to others, but that is the way it is. Of course, it is as true for your competition as for you. The thing to keep in mind is not to let this be blown up in your imagination to the point of obsession. Moreover, this is the reason why *your* superior will make every effort to keep control over most of your contacts with those responsible for promotion into middle management.

How Was Your Last Performance Review?

Whether your enterprise uses a formal or an informal method of performance reviews, we can assume that yours have been above average ever since you entered supervision. If this were not so, you would hardly be a serious candidate for promotion now. You have established in the thinking of managers above you a pattern of managerial behavior with certain recognized strengths and weaknesses. Moreover, you must have been making significant progress in shoring up your weaknesses—at least enough to convince your superior that you are making progress. Hopefully, by now you are the principal architect of your development program, both short and long range. You have explored many approaches to improving yourself, with consistently better results from some than from the others. Your interaction with the management development specialist in your organization is, hopefully, becoming both a friendship and a professional relationship. You have maintained adequate or better mastery of your particular discipline, while at the same time learning the theory and practice of supervision at an accelerating rate.

All these processes of growth are standard prerequisites for a candidate for promotion into middle management. You probably know several other men who have also completed these basics satisfactorily. Whether you or one of them will actually be chosen to fill the next vacancy in the higher echelon will narrow itself in large measure on the basis of your recent performance in critical areas of supervision. In other words, you are keeping at peak performance everything concerning your present job, *while still demonstrating a desirable growth pattern.*

One element of performance which both you and your superior should scrutinize closely is the matter of recent innovation you have introduced, whether it was implemented in your own crew, or designed and recommended for someone else. The evaluation of the results of this new procedure should be mercilessly rigorous. Remember that change for change's sake is one of the most sterile and useless exercises any business can undergo. Your ability as an idea man must be quantified by the payoff of the successful innovations, rather than by the sheer number of ideas you spin off from an active mind. It is the same line of reasoning you use when you build the concept of quality into judgments of your subordinates' productivity.

Another area for searching study is your performance in cost control. Your fiscal responsibilities will be increased several times when you assume your higher duties. The first-line supervisor is basically responsible for the production of a product or of services, whereas the middle manager is the watchdog of the enterprise's moneybags. What he spends or does not spend in running his part of the action will largely determine the amount of profit shown in the annual report. The trick is to spend money wisely to get a fair return on its use. Many managers flunk the entire course when they perceive themselves as misers holding tightly to the purse strings, and letting go of a dollar only after a Herculean struggle. This is not the way modern managements operate. The key to success is the healthy cash flow the corporation can show, with the concomitant generation of a reasonable profit.

You should by now be deep into the consideration (if not the actual practice) of the proper capital outlay needed to make your part of the department more modern, more productive, and more profitable. You will need some sage guidance here. If he is wise, your own superior will recognize some limitations of his own, and steer you to contact with the financial men of your company, so that you can learn from their advice, and make a better showing in your own performance.

It must not be inferred from these statements that you will have given up any of your attention to production as such. You will still ultimately stand or fall on whether you are able to get out your quotas on time at a reasonable cost. Hopefully, some of your developmental training will show its effects in a better and richer relationship with the people you supervise. You should be finding it continually easier to reach your goals through the improved performance of your crew. Also, they will have increased their commitment to and involvement with the organization's goals, so that their individual contributions will be more meaningful and constructive.

As you examine your thinking about your last performance review, you must feel free to touch bases with your superior, to be sure that your evaluations agree with his. Complete candor should be employed by both of you. Anything less will result in some foggy communications and misunderstandings that could be fatal to your hopes. Of course, a failure on your part at this point would be catastrophic for your boss as well; he is putting a whole pile of his chips on your success because you are his protégé. This interlocking relationship between the mutual success of superior and subordinate is often overlooked by managers, to their ultimate extreme discomfiture. The superior is judged at least as much on the success of those who work for him as he is on what he does himself. This is one of the responsibilities of any manager.

If you have any lingering doubt as to where you stand at this moment, don't hesitate to ask your superior for a special performance review—in full-dress formality. Lay out the entire book, and read it page by page. Your perusal of it together will reassure you that your conclusions are the same, no matter on what part of the continuum they lie. A last-minute recognition of a shortcoming will give you a mathematical chance of correcting it before the final judgment is rendered, and before someone else beats you to the wire and the laurel wreath.

Is Your Boss in Your Corner?

Throughout this book, we have assumed that your immediate superior is the strongest supporter for your promotion into middle management. Practically all of your development program has been designed around this concept, and based on the expectation that he will bend every effort to help you in its realization. This is not to say that you could not have sponsors more powerful than he, higher up on the management line. Certainly there have been many cases where promotions have been made over the active opposition of the immediate superior, but this does not happen with any great frequency, and it is the hard way to achieve your goal. If you have the slightest doubt about the active support of your boss for your promotion, you should run an immediate check to determine what the situation really is. You dare not have any errors in your calculation at this stage of the game. A misreading of his position would be fatal, if you have built your campaign around him.

Most assuredly, the best way to find out where your superior stands is to ask him directly. If he has any of the elements of decency, he will answer your questions directly and completely. If the final outcome shows his attitude to be negative, you must at once fall back, and design and begin to implement a new campaign strategy. This would mean a serious delay and perhaps some extra training and development work to overcome some of the weaknesses your superior claims to see in your makeup. Also involved would be the recruitment and signing up of a new sponsor strong enough to do the job and willing to take on a direct confrontation with your superior.

These two criteria are sometimes difficult to meet satisfactorily. The fact that your superior may have given you a final negative on the issue of his support does not mean that you should not pay attention to the rationale he advances for his decision. He may have a valid reservation or two about your readiness, and if this is so, he would be doing you a big favor to refuse you his support. Remember always that he has ego involvement in the total situation. There is no middle ground available for the effect of your advancement on his career, one way or the other. If you are successful, you are a huge credit entry in his managerial ledger; if you fail, you may have seriously wounded his chances for further promotion. Naturally, he can be mistaken in the value judgments he makes concerning this issue, and he would be the first to admit this possibility.

Let us revert to our ongoing assumption that your superior is fundamentally your greatest fan. In these last moments before your actual promotion, you should make every available use of his support. This can be done by giving him many subtle cues that will trigger him into activity. The two of you, both individually and jointly, should see opportunities to pursue in the game of capturing your promotion; frequent strategy huddles are called for, and should be used. Nor should the two of you be alone at this stage in the game. Remember, you have been cultivating and using political cohorts for some time now, and never has there been a more clear-cut call for concerted action than at this point. It is probable that there will be no explicitly designated leadership for this period. If ever a team effort were called for, this is it. The rumor or actual appearance of a desirable vacancy in the hierarchy is the signal to you and your buddies to make the last effort to get you the job.

We said there would probably be no established leadership, but it is clear that your boss should be the communications center for passing information during this time. He is tactically in the best position for effecting instant message sending and message receiving at a time when speed is of the greatest urgency. Moreover, his higher position in the organization give him quicker access to those who will be making the final decision. You will be furiously active with your job, your development program, and your political activity, and you can't for a moment afford to neglect any of these facets of the total.

Of prime importance, naturally, is the receipt of any

communications or signals you get from above. You must remain totally alert to any cue you get; no one will be repeating them, and your reception of the first sending must be clean and sure. Neither will you be given much time for interpreting and analyzing them. You are in a situation of constant and continuing testing, and your future is the stakes of the game. Time compression will be so great that you must make one smooth process of the receipt of communication, its reading and interpretation, and the ensuing action, with no perceptible break between any two segments.

* * *

At this time in your career, communication from your superior assumes a new and overriding importance. Because of this, you must be especially careful in what you send to him. There must not be too much, but every item of any importance must be transmitted instantly. He can do little to help you unless he is in possession of all relevant data. Your analysis of his signals to you is critical; this is no time for a major error in interpretation. One of the more important phases is the number and kind of his intimations of your approaching promotion. These will not always be overt; you must be particularly sensitive to the things he cannot, or will not, say to you now.

The signal service your superior can perform for you is to keep clear and unclogged your communication channels upward. The executive echelon must be apprised of your progress and activities; they cannot make judgments in a vacuum. Concurrently, you are required to keep your day-to-day performance impeccable. Finally, you need to know whether your boss is really with you.

11

Now What Do You Do?

PART of this book has sounded like a training manual for an athlete. The analogy is good; the athlete learns early in his career what his strong points are, and so must you, the manager, if you are to be a winner in the business games. Individual differences account for the fact that supervisors display a variety of strengths. One man will excel in planning, while another will shine in interpersonal relationships and qualities of leadership. Some men are demons at control; others will constantly be able to come up with the most functional of organizations for a given set of circumstances. It is this variety of strong points which makes the managerial race so close and interesting. As the race proceeds, one or the other of the areas of management practices will become more important than the rest.

How Do You Maximize Your Assets?

Your purpose here is to determine your assets beyond any doubt, and then to capitalize on them. A review of your performance appraisals is a point of entry for this study. Your superior is in a much better position than your peers to evaluate where you are, and if his appraisal has been honest, you will have notation and documentation of his observations.

You have already been advised not to neglect a strength in order to concentrate on correcting a weakness. Neglected muscles will atrophy. All your muscles must be exercised so that development be symmetrical. Only the amount of time and effort on a strength and a weakness will vary, but both must receive some attention. It is a human characteristic that we like to do those things we do well. When your associates notice your enthusiasm and energetic approach, they will respond by being more eager and productive. In other words, you can accomplish more because of the cooperation evoked by your obvious expertise. It would be foolish not to make use of your extra ability. You can get the whole job done quickly and more productively by concentrating on your elements of worthy performance. By operating this way, you will also be taking advantage of another psychological truism. When you have conditioned those about you to expect superior performance from you in a given part of your job, the maintenance of this superiority becomes easier as a function of their belief in your ability. An operative system, once constructed and put into use, will continue to function with a minimum amount of care.

Your friends will help you to maximize your assets by turning to you for aid in their problems in these categories. This extra activity offers both mental reinforcement and propitious practice. You should make all reasonable efforts to cooperate with these demands on your time, for your personal benefit and for the good of the enterprise. More than that, you will be putting capital into the bank of friendship, to remain on call for repayment in kind later. This free trade between colleagues is an exhibition of the highest sort of professionalism. It raises the climate and general tone of the area, which will enhance everyone's morale. From a broad viewpoint, the net results will be gains for the enterprise, as well as for several supervisors and their crews. It is by this method that organizations come to be known as strong. If you can emerge as one of the leaders in an operating department, where the general performance is far above average, your chances for promotion are materially increased. Success feeds and grows on success.

One benefit of this cycle will be observable growth and development among your people. Your position of leadership among them will elicit noticeable amounts of copying of your actions. When they see you profit from the way you do things, they will immediately make a transfer of learning to their own operation. As the old saw has it, imitation is the sincerest form of flattery. Good passing first-string quarterbacks are likely to have good passing understudies.

Maximization of gains from this practice will occur when you make frequent assessments of your position for purposes of comparison. Of course, rather than stopping to look back at your gains, you will glance over your shoulder while you keep on running. You should build a book on your own performance as carefully as you would on that of your closest competitor. Remember, too, that your standards of comparison are changeable. What was passable a year ago will of necessity be substandard today. The key to this process is alertness. Its twin, sensitivity, will act as a backup for making necessary value judgments, and will help to verify results.

At this point, you are roughly at the close of your adolescence as a manager. Your imminent promotion will put you squarely in the middle of a group of men. Your youthfulness may be appreciated; youthful behavior will never be tolerated. This should not be a source of anxiety, because you will have the advantages of your chronological youth going for you in terms of greater strength, more stamina, better resilience, and probably more adaptability to change. While older managers take time out to determine their course of action, you can start down the track well ahead of them with the change absorbed and implemented in your crew's activities. You may become known as a young Turk, but you will have gained the respect of your peers during the action.

Of course, your greatest adjustment will have to be made to the new job itself. Your entire milieu will have changed. Your physical surroundings will be different, and you will have truly become the occupant of an office, rather than a transient in a cubbyhole. Your staff people will be much more demanding of your time, and they will be in direct competition with your line subordinates. Be sure that you don't slight the needs of either group under the greater pressures of this strange situation.

How Do You Minimize Your Liabilities?

Although you have been working hard at eliminating your weaknesses, it is unlikely that you have shored them up sufficiently to make them equal to your strengths. They will still be there to give you trouble at critical times. Most people tend to compensate for this by covering their weaknesses with their strengths. If a tennis player has a weak backhand, he will play more of the court to his forehand, even if this means that he has to run further and harder. If a manager finds it consistently difficult to plan well, he will be forced to depend more on directing and controlling to cover for his sketchy planning. Of course, this may give him the reputation of being a fire fighter, which is not good, but at least he can stall for time while he strengthens his planning ability. Tactically, he should throw his strong defenses around his areas of liability, and push all offensive action through the media of his assets. This will result in a less well-balanced performance, but his net results will be better than they would if he equalized his action.

This situation calls for hard-nosed analysis at regular intervals. You must know where you stand competitively at all times. Your competition will be doing this, and you will be leaving yourself wide open unless you follow suit. This is one of the areas where young managers frequently have trouble. They have been indoctrinated as to the nature and caliber of the competition outside the organization, but the idea that their stiffest struggle will be with other members of their own enterprise is often hard to sell. The commonplaceness of your acquaintances and friends at work can be delusive, if you do not allow yourself to recognize their ambitions and efforts to grow, which will

NOW WHAT DO YOU DO?

be at least as great as yours if they are aspiring. Good old George may be burning more midnight oil than you are, and could be the sleeper in the race for the next promotion.

One of the better ways to minimize your liabilities is to admit to them openly and frankly to your superior, and to those of your associates you trust explicitly. Discuss your drawbacks. Get others' opinions on ways to attack them. Call in your political committee for an executive session of planning for your development program. This openness will disarm your critics, and will reinforce your friends' admiration of your fitness as a manager. The fact that you are aware of your problems, and are doing something about them, just might turn out to be your strongest asset in the overall race. Above all, avail yourself of the advice and counsel of the management development people in your organization. Their analysis of your problems will probably be much more professional than will that of your lay friends and colleagues, although you should not hesitate to get them all into the act.

A critical factor of playing down your weaknesses will be the rigid control you maintain about your attitude toward them. It is mandatory that you do *not* become panicky after you have made an analysis. Always keep in mind the fact that others have soft spots as well, even if they are not the same as yours. They, too, will be facing their moments of truth as they assess their positions, and there is none so strong that he can afford to be complacent. But it would be better to be complacent than to go to pieces from frustration and fright after you have cast up the accounts. Self-control has never been more important to you than at this moment—woo it like a mistress!

The need for maintaining a vigorous record of the feedback you get during this exercise cannot be overemphasized. Others can almost always see your weaknesses more clearly than you can. If they are friendly enough to give you a cue, appreciate it, and make use of the information in whatever way is indicated. More often than not, the key pieces to the jigsaw puzzle can be uncovered from information given you by your friends and fellow workers. The important thing is to keep a running record of their inputs, and to spend some time analyzing them for content and implied direction.

This is another occasion when you should make the effort to extend your comparisons beyond your own organization, to find out what the situation is among some of your friends in other businesses. Is your personal situation typical or atypical of what is going on there? Are your liabilities commonly shared with others, or do you find yourself in a relatively small group? What are they doing to ameliorate their problems? Are you missing something in the way of corrective action? Is there a new technique which has slipped by you and which is giving them help when needed most? These are important questions to you; get their answers to the best of your ability, and build them into your plans for growth. Remember, your entire perspective must be broadened from here on out, and this is an excellent place to start that process.

These last days of your residence in the lower echelons of management are of course traumatic to you. The needles on the pressure gauges are rising bit by bit almost every day. Will you or won't you get the nod? Has all this effort been in vain? The answer to the latter question is an unqualified no, even if you are not promoted. The increased efficiency on your present job, the enlargement of its scope, the greater responsibility you have assumed voluntarily, the increased contacts you have made with, and your greater understanding of, the executive level, can only combine to make your job as a supervisor more satisfying to you. The changing world in which we live demands constant adjustment. We must grow, or we shall die. The man who stands still has just announced that he has quit the race, and it will be difficult for him to maintain his present position, because there are too many behind him who are not standing still. Of course, this is a defeatist attitude you can never adopt; it is too foreign to your nature, and would negate everything you have done to remain competitive. If you are not chosen for this promotion, another will always come along.

How Do You Force-Feed Your Growth?

Management as a way of life is a matter of time pressures. You have never known a period since you became a supervisor when you had enough time to do all the things required of you. You have resorted to a system of priorities, and have done those tasks which were absolutely imperative, while leaving other items to be picked up as you could. The only thing which keeps you afloat under this method of operation is the fact that all other managers are forced to adopt the same plan, so at least you can remain competitive, if not exactly happy with the compromise you have had to make.

This matter carries over into your development program. You tailored it on a periodic basis to your evident needs, with the help of your superior and the experts in the field, only to discover that the available time didn't cover everything you had detailed to be done. You took the same course here that you did in your general management activities—you decided which were the mandatory items, took care of them, and postponed the others to a later time. Some of these, you discovered to your chagrin, are still being postponed. At this turning point in your career, you would do well to take another hard look at these neglected growth elements, and make some major decisions about them. Are they still as important to you as you considered them to be when you built them into your program? If they are, you will have to do something about them now, or be aware that you are leaving some gaping holes in your growth pattern, at a time when you need every tool available to get the job done and to be ready for advancement. The most frustrating and humiliating thing that could happen to you would be to miss your promotion, and know why you did and how it could have been prevented. Now is when you go all out to remedy the obvious lacks.

If the missing elements require you to absent yourself from the job for a time, do it. The temptation now is to begin to think of yourself as the indispensable man, and that is still as much of a fallacy as it ever was. An absence now will not only enable you to accomplish your objective of the desired expansion activity, but will also give you the chance to test your planning ability, your powers of delegation, and the state of development of your understudy on the job. Give him the package, including the authority to act, and go about your business of personal development with a clear head and an untroubled mind. If you have picked the right man to take your place, things will go ahead normally; if you have not, it is high time you found it out and did something about it before it is too late. Your management will have a tendency to go along with your recommendation for a replacement for you; it will be sad if it appears almost at once that your choice is poor.

The word at this juncture for your growth exercises is concentration. The process, the time, and the effort involved will be useless unless you bend all your thoughts to the problem at hand, and effect a quick and positive result in the desired area. You most certainly have no time to waste; make your investment pay off by your single-minded attack. One of the most heartening results of all will be the exhilaration that comes from a change of scene, meeting new people, and the interactions you will have with others from different scenes. This will happen whatever your choice of area or subject of study. The content is, of course, important, but equally so is this feeling of newness in both surroundings and personal associations. You should come away from one of these sessions not only with new ideas and techniques, but also with some valuable new friends with whom you will want to keep in touch during the rest of your career.

It is entirely possible that your most pressing neglected growth activities are such that you will not have to actually leave the job to deal with them. They may be so closely job related that you can take care of them only at work. This, in a sense, complicates the matter, because it is always hard to work one of these projects into your regular day. There are too many distractions and interruptions. Again, it will take your best concentration to accomplish your goals. Remember that if a tool is to be useful to you, the time and effort required for its forging are worth it.

Concomitant with this second effort at development activity is the necessity for especially good communications up the line. Your superior must be meticulously advised both about the nature of your exercises and about the progress you are making. He is still the center of your upward interactions; his interpretations and assent will be sought by the executive level to confirm your general readiness for promotion.

At this point, you are starting to become a change agent for a much greater segment of the organization. Up to now, your influence on change has rested almost entirely with the people reporting to you; from here on out, your activities will also cause reactions in those above you. The new things you learn and put into effect in your crew will be evaluated by your management for possible adoption elsewhere. Obvious successes will be reported in many other working groups, and you can expect to see some copying of your efforts. This is fine. So long as you receive credit as the originator, it is naturally desirable that the good be spread as far as possible through the organization. You are still working for the enterprise first, and yourself second. This is the way of the professional manager. Your own future will never be hurt if you follow this general guideline.

Our frequent references to your development program throughout this volume have been intentional. It is the foundation on which your career rests, and your success will be a measure of its authenticity and correctness. But your promotion into middle management will not obviate its future necessity. You will need to continue it just to maintain your position, let alone your progress.

What Channels Are Open to You?

We have indicated that many needs may become apparent in your development program. You have recognized some of these for a long time, but have not had a chance to work on them. Others have only appeared as felt needs when the possibility of promotion became more imminent.

As you consider these needs, and begin to search for ways to satisfy them, one thing should be perfectly clear: There is no channel or resource within the company which can be legally or morally denied to you in order to gain your objective of proper growth. If your company management is honest and sincere in its stated policy of doing everything it can to aid its employees to develop themselves, all avenues are yours to command. Of course, some company policies will necessitate your showing a need to know to the proper official. Once done, however, he should not be reticent in giving you the desired information. This is true whatever the area or function involved, and whatever the data—financial, personnel, or proprietary in the extreme. By this time, you have long since established your trustworthiness; if you should betray that trust, you will have thrown overboard every vestige of hope for promotion.

Naturally, you will not abuse this right during your preparation for advancement. Only you really know when you have the information you need to gain a new perspective on the job you will be occupying. It may seem to others that you are becoming a nuisance, but this is not the time for you to give evidence of tender sensibilities. Get what you need, and let impatient or unperceptive managers think what they will. The ones who really count will know what you are doing, and will commend you for it.

We should not leave the impression that all the information you will need is to be found within your enterprise. If you have not already done so, you should explore in depth all outside avenues to memory banks of pertinent data. The mechanical accumulation and storage of information has become so awesomely efficient that it staggers the imagination. Your job at the moment is to find the small group of specialists who can help guide you. Usually, these people are by function, if not by title, technical librarians of many sorts. If you can describe properly what you are seeking, the probability is high that they can locate it for you quickly. Since the advent of the time-sharing computer, the smaller company is rapidly narrowing the advantage of the larger one. If you work for a medium-size or small enterprise, and if it subscribes to such a service, you are as close as your telephone to the new information you need. Your job will be to determine which data are pertinent to your problems. Since the development of electronic data processing, many a promising manager has been drowned in a sea of irrelevant data.

The major metropolitan areas now have services which will make the search, write either a short précis or a complete report, and return you the package—for a price. If you can afford it, employ these services, either through the company or personally if management refuses to finance you. Possibly your time is now more valuable to you than the money involved. It goes without saying that the gathering of this information is totally useless unless you make constructive use of it afterward. Although you may have begun a more or less textbook exercise in development, the acid test of your real growth will be seen in how well you make practical applications of the new knowledge.

The goal of this entire procedure is to start working you more firmly into the scientific area of modern management. It is still true that today's manager must operate within a dichotomy of half science and half art, but the trend toward using more scientific methods in management is clearly evident, and its slope is increasing. The time will come when a small segment of the manager's job will be artistic in nature, and that will have to do with personnel matters of running the job. Some managers find extremely traumatic the realization that the base of their job is shifting. It gives them a feeling of insecurity which certain people cannot live with. If you can learn to endure this fact at the moment of your entry into middle management, you will have a tremendous advantage over your peers. As we have said repeatedly, middle managment is the stronghold of those who strive desperately to maintain the status quo. This is one element of it they will not be able to maintain; if you recognize it, you are miles ahead of your competition.

Because technology has proliferated so rapidly, and has become correspondingly more complex, the channels you will need to examine have multiplied prodigiously. By the time you read this book, many new techniques and methods will have been invented, each with its own esoteric body of knowledge, and each with a vocabulary you will have to learn before the method can become useful to you. The mechanics alone will absorb a significant part of your time for the rest of your business career. You dare not neglect them; your value judgments of their potential usefulness to you will be the touchstone for determining your future actions in each of the areas involved.

Don't forget that another change involved with becoming a middle manager will be much more neglect of you personally by your new bosses. Executives have a way of assuming that middle managers are big boys, and can effectively take care of themselves. You will have to inure yourself to learning to disturb them only with Class-A problems and emergencies; for the rest, you will be on your own.

In any event, this should be one of the most frustrating, and at the same time the most fulfilling, times of your life. There are so many fascinating trails to explore, each with its promise of an El Dorado at the end, that you will have difficulty in choosing the most viable. Comparison and selection will become a way of life for you.

Can You See the Chance?

Unless you believe you have a reasonable chance for promotion in the near future, everything we have said in this book will have been totally useless, and will only add to your general frustration and unhappiness. Although it could be argued cogently that a full-dress development program is a must for any manager, you were preparing for a shot at a particular goal: promotion into middle management. You will naturally, then, be on the qui vive for any opportunity which may present itself to achieve this goal. A common mistake many first-line supervisors make is to acquire tunnel vision while looking up their present line of progression. Although a majority of promotions occur within a given department, it is also true that vacancies or new positions may exist elsewhere. It is understood why you might wish to become a middle manager in a familiar area; there are some definite advantages to being promoted across functional or departmental lines. The simple knowledge that you are in a completely unknown area will act as an extra stimulus to the betterment of your overall performance. At least, there will be small danger of failure from overconfidence. In most cases, you will be required to learn one or more disciplines previously unknown to you, since it is quite customary for a middle manager to be in charge of two or more different functions.

Your search for a possible promotional berth should be vigorous and unremitting. Some of the better positions never receive any publicity at all until the new jobholder is announced. This is one of the times when it is important to you to have a network of friendly correspondents in other departments. Strategically placed secretaries can give you a real boost, if they are friendly to you. A few days' advance warning of a planned change may alter your entire career, if it means that you are the first to make a discreet contact with the hiring executive. He will seldom push hard to find the source of your information; the fact that you have it will attest to your alertness and interest. Let those less gifted wait to be summoned to the presence. You are already aware of the fact that in this kind of situation, considerable finesse is required. You can botch the whole business by an indelicate or uncouth approach.

Some men have benefitted spectacularly from their own inventiveness and creativity. If you can conceptualize a new organizational structure, there just might be a slot for you in its middle management, so long as you can defend the rationale for the structure. It is commonly understood among management people that a man fashions his own job once put in the slot, but it adds a nice touch to have him dream up the position in the first place.

Another good chance for advancement may lie in the field of new projects. If your company operates under this system, mine that area assiduously. With the start-up of any new project, many new middle management positions are invariably created. Even if you know when entering it that the project will have a short life, you may want to go in, because you will at least gain the experience of being in a middle manager's job, and company executives are not prone to take this background lightly when looking over a prospect. It just might be that a short-term residency in middle management could pay off at long odds later.

There is one benefit to project life: The atmosphere and orientation are superb for innovative and imaginative managers, and continued excitement best describes the climate. Some find this environment difficult to live with, but most young managers are intrigued by the surroundings, and thrive on them. Here, the effort has to be made to secure enough time from a new and unstructured job to pay enough attention to what is going on in the entire environment. If you *can* do it, you will widen the white water between you and your competition.

Your coming of age as a manager will occur during your stay in the middle area. The process of maturation is not easy for anyone. Its base is change; its vehicle is trauma; its final form will come close to describing you as a manager from here on. Make your existence in the middle echelons productive for yourself as well as for the company. At this point, and beyond, what happens to you as a person also happens to the company, because you give so much of yourself that you become almost physically grafted onto the managerial tree of your enterprise.

This is one period in your work life which will seem quite novel to you, and at the same time will leave a hint of déjà vu. You have seen it before—when you were looking industriously for your first job. The fact that it is set in a pictorial representation of what your company does for you should not frighten you. This is not the first time such a blatant attempt has been made to brainwash you. Of course, it is only when the event (or events) thoroughly intrigue you that you can start to bank the attendant bag of sweets. The combination of new and old at this point is particularly felicitous, for it will facilitate your settling in to your sphere of heavier responsibility, authority, accountability—and influence.

Both neophytes and old pros inhabit this land in abundance. What they learn will be conditioned by their own activities and perceptions.

How Far Is Up?

You have come a long way since that day when you first decided it might be nice to be a supervisor. There was a big change in orientation to accomplish, some intensive training to undergo, and a hectic introduction into a new world. Somehow, you survived these hurdles, managed to land on your feet, and took command of the situation. Then there came a fine period of growth in your experience as a first-line supervisor. You learned many things— some of them the hard way. Head bumping with professionals at head bumping became a way of life; some you lost, but more you won. You saw your people weld themselves into an effective group capable of getting the job done quickly and economically. Your management people learned to trust your judgment, and to respect you as a responsible manager.

Roughly at the time these things had been accomplished, there came a reawakening of your ambition to do better for yourself. You heard the siren call of the unknown land of middle management, with all its mysteries and unexplored bypaths. With the help of your superior and some of your friends in higher echelons, you were able to shed some light on these unknown areas, and what you saw reinforced your desire to get yourself into this kind of job.

Then began the long and arduous period of preparation, with a carefully designed and meticulously implemented development program. Some new elements were introduced; among them were the concept of supervising multiple disciplines and the necessity for growth in your ability to conceptualize. The satisfaction of these needs was undoubtedly a disturbing experience. Some of the concepts seemed to be in direct opposition to principles which you had held sacrosanct all your life. It was hard to graft them onto your philosophy and build them into your managerial life. The fact that you could do this was one of the first tests of your eligibility to become a middle manager. There now remains the question of what to expect from the future.

Obviously the first consideration is to master your new job as a middle manager. It is sufficiently more complex than your previous assignment to offer a challenge to the fullest extent of your capacity. At times you will be certain that the cause is lost, and you will wonder whether it would be possible to slip back into the relatively safe position of the first-line supervisor. Fortunately, these periods of self-doubt will be short lived, and you will be able to maintain the impetus you have generated. Almost before you know it, you will be comfortable and productive as a respected member of middle management.

At this point will come another career decision. Will this be the end of the climb? Will the atmosphere here be rarefied enough so that you won't want to put on an oxygen mask for the climb to the final heights? The rewards you are now receiving are not inconsiderable, and you can expect them to increase satisfactorily during the years ahead. You will be widely hailed and respected as a solid citizen, both by your peers and by the general public. Many department heads and directors have prestige and job status enough to satisfy them for the rest of their lives. Your ongoing, exciting feeling of participation in the real world of running your enterprise will bring you a lot of personal satisfaction. Through your company political affiliations, you may even grow into the position of kingmaker, with its concomitant secret satisfactions.

This decision is yours alone to make. If you opt to go on, you will encounter some awesome novel responsibilities and demands. Suffice it to say that sometimes the choice is not as real as it appears—some are driven inexorably onward, even against their conscious volition. For those hag-ridden by ambition, there is no choice, but only a decision as to which road leads to the future.

So You Want to Be a Manager!

* * *

The question of what to do in the closing days of your supervisory experience poses some special problems. First, you want and need to make the best possible use of those assets you were born with or have arduously developed over the years. You will want to apply the principle of maximizing your assets, concurrently with that of minimizing your liabilities. Even at the sacrifice (temporarily) of the development of a well-rounded personality, expediency says you must make the most adept use possible of what you currently have going for you.

Of equal importance is the unequivocal need to force-feed your growth in preparation for the possible promotion. No one else can do this for you. It is not a function to be delegated to a dedicated staff man. You know what you need; you alone can go out and do whatever is necessary to take you off the hook.

Happily, several channels are open to you in the accomplishment of this task. You will be held accountable for the performance of these duties—why not get into it at the earliest possible moment, so that the experience you gain here can be meaningful to you in later years?

Lastly, it is mandatory that you recognize the situation, plus the responsible management, with an open mind, and be prepared to go all out to accomplish your ends in the long run.

Directly in line with these points is this one: You are going to prepare for deciding between remaining where you are and working for another promotion to the executive level. This decision involves the final career choice of your life as a manager.

Index

Action initiation
  level of, 28–34
  management philosophy and, 31
  managerial grid and, 30
Adaptability, in middle manager, 40–42
Administration, knowledge of in first-line supervisor, 4
Administrative record, promotability and, 152–153
Adrenaline, stress and, 19
After-hours work, tolerance for, 22–25
Alliances, in management politics, 112–115
Allies, in development planning, 124–125
Ambition
  balance sheet for, 37
  in first-line supervisor, 1, 16, 244
  in late bloomer, 35
  level of, 35–38
  as major factor in career, 16
  preparedness needed for, 35
Anxiety, business ethics and, 106–107

Anxiety level, leadership style and, 192–194
Assets, maximization of, 227–229

Background information, from superior, 210–211
Blake, Robert R., 30 n., 64
Boss
    avoidance of, 32–34
    as father figure, 33
    see also Superior
Business ethics
    anxiety and, 106–107
    code of, 103–106

Change
    anticipated, 93
    impending, 93–95
    reaction time in, 93–95
    vs. status quo, 43, 80–82
Changing work force, leadership style and, 197–200
Character assassination, 118
Check sheets, 57
"Colleague," vs. "subordinate," 101–102
Communications
    cost control in, 220–221
    feedback in, 168
    first-line supervisor and, 3
    leadership and, 189
    management problems and policies in, 210–211
    middle manager's abilities in, 57
    from superior, 205–225
    superior as kingpin in, 215–216
    trust and, 168
Company politics, 100–120
    wife in, 158
    see also Politics
Competition
    in management politics, 117–120
    from peers, 26
    promotability and, 144–145
    and responsibility, 26
Compromise, art of, 87–90
Concentration, in executive growth, 235

INDEX

Conceptualization, ability in, 112–113
Conceptual skills, in middle manager, 46–48
Confidence of subordinates, *see* Trust
Conflict, resolution of among subordinates, 63–67
Cooperation
   in peer relationships, 170–173
   selfish motives in, 171
Coordination factor, in middle manager, 56–58
Cost control, performance review in, 5–7, 220
Creativity, promotability and, 241

Decentralization, middle manager and, 44–45
Decision making
   management politics and, 111–112
   pressure and, 20
Delegation, by middle manager, 49–52
Detail work, homework and, 22–25
Development goals, time limit in, 123
Development plan
   allies in, 124–125
   "building vs. repairing" in, 125–127
   comparison standards in, 124
   force-feeding in, 233–236
   functional requirement in, 127–128
   growth needs in, 132–135, 233–236
   help in, 135–138
   job perspective in, 134
   and Management by Objectives, 129
   minimal time limits in, 139
   minimizing of liabilities in, 231
   monitoring in, 130
   on-the-job experience and, 135
   peer relationships in, 130
   personal discipline in, 123
   personal relationships in, 128
   perspective in, 128–129
   plateaus in, 131
   preparation of, 122–125
   present state of, 121–141
   reinforcement in, 126
   roadblocks in, 125–126

Development plan *(cont.)*
  self-analysis in, 132–133
  self-confidence and, 132
  self-control in, 231
  seminars in, 136–137
  sensitivity training in, 132–133
  superior's cooperation in, 136
  time schedule in, 138–140
  value judgments in, 141
Disapproval, by middle manager, 85
Disciplines, new, 53–54
Double standard, in peer relationships, 103

Emotion, as handicap in executive action, 177
Employee relations, importance of, 7
  see also Peer relationships
Enemies
  attitude toward, 176–179
  information about, 175
  in peer relationships, 173–176
Ethics
  in middle management, 103–105
  of price fixing, 106
Executive action, disapproval of, 85
  see also Action initiation
Executive potential, in management politics, 113–114

Feelings, dissembling of, 163–164, 178
First-line supervisor
  administrative skills of, 4
  ambition in, 1, 16, 244
  ambition level of, 35–38
  avoidance of boss by, 32–34
  career choices and future prospects for, 243–246
  communication in, 3
  employee relations and, 7
  front-office contacts and, 156
  group productivity and, 5
  homework by, 22–25
  increased responsibility for, 34–35
  industrial psychology use by, 27
  job-enrichment techniques for, 11–14

INDEX

First-line supervisor *(cont.)*
  "job stretching" in, 8–11, 161
  knowledge of company by, 3, 46
  leadership and, 8, 202 *(see also* Leadership)
  managerial style and, 2–3
  opportunities facing, 237–241
  pressures and responsibilities of, 19–21
  production costs and, 5–7, 220
  production standards and, 5
  product quality and, 6
  promotion planning for, 16–17, 121–141
  public relations and, 7
  routine performance in, 8
  "security" of, 2
  squabbling by, 25–26
  things learned by, 1–4
  work force and, 2
  see also Middle manager; Promotability
Flexibility, promotability and, 147
Friendship
  cooperation and, 172
  of peers, 164
  tabulation of, 165
  trust and, 167
Front-office contacts, promotability and, 155–159

Goals
  manager's commitment to, 61–62
  superior's control in, 32–33
  see also Development plan; Management by Objectives
Good will
  of peer group, 149
  and promotability, 149
Grievances, promotability and, 148, 152
Group
  evaluation of manager by, 116
  status of manager in, 148–150
  study of by middle manager, 90–93
Group effectiveness, leadership style and, 191
Group status, measurement of, 150–152

Growth
    asset maximizing and, 228
    concentration in, 235
    force-feeding of, 233–236
Growth plan, *see* Development plan

Harvard Business Review, 11 n.
Health, overtime and homework as factors in, 24
Heart attacks, pressure as cause of, 19, 97
Herzberg, Frederick, 11, 13
High blood pressure, 97
Homework
    by first-line or middle manager, 22–25
    health and, 24
Hostility, in peer relationships, 174

Industrial psychology, use of by first-line supervisor, 27
Information
    background, 210–211
    manager's need for, 238
Innovation
    management politics and, 112
    in middle manager, 39
Insecurity, unfriendliness and, 25
Interdepartmental relationships, 48–49
Interpersonal relationships
    job pressure and, 98
    promotability and, 147
    see also Peer relationships

Jealousy
    in management politics, 117–119
    in subordinate, 67–68
Job challenge, 8–11
Job development and growth, 121–141
Job enrichment, need for, 11–14
Job excitement, generation of, 10
Job performance, review of, 159
Job perspective, in development plan, 134
Job status, evaluation of, 14
"Job stretching," in first-line supervisor, 8–10, 161

Late bloomer, ambition in, 35

INDEX

Leadership
  acknowledgment of, 195
  action initiation and, 29
  communication and, 189
  promotability and, 147
  shortcomings in, 8
  status and dignity of, 202
  testing of, 201–202
Leadership style, 30, 183–204
  anxiety level in, 192–194
  changing work force and, 197–200
  confidence and trust in, 187–190
  group efficiency and, 191
  growth and, 200–204
  "locked in" state of, 184–187
  new employees and, 198
  peer's attitude toward, 194–197
  and promotion, 186
  self-control and, 193
  self-development and, 200–204
  subordinate's view of, 190–192
Learning
  politics and, 116
  process of in middle manager, 49
Liabilities, minimizing of, 230–233
Loyalty, management politics and, 108

Machiavellianism, 100–105
Management
  action initiation in, 28–29
  delegation in, 50–51
  ethics in, 103–105
  first-line supervisor and, 3–7
  managing of other managers in, 50
  operating rules in, 105–107
  politics of, 100–120
  scientific aspects of, 239
  social responsibility of, 106
Management by Objectives, 70–73
  development plan and, 129
  as group project, 72
  organizational aspects of, 73

Management by Objectives, 70–73 *(cont.)*
   promotability and, 143
Management philosophy
   action initiation and, 31
   consonance with, 143
   from superior, 211
   supervisor action and, 31
Management politics
   alliances in, 112–115
   competition in, 117–120
   decision making and, 111–112
   innovation and, 112
   jealousy in, 117–119
   learning and, 116
   loyalty and, 108
   opposition to superior in, 110
   upward mobility and, 111
Manager
   business ethics and, 103–107
   compromise type, 65
   confrontation type, 65
   "country club" type, 64
   development plan of, 121–141
   differences among, 60–63
   emotional handicap in, 177
   goal commitment of, 61–62
   "great gray abdicator" type, 64
   group's rating of, 148–151
   as human being, 61
   impact of on subordinates, 190–192
   individuality in, 62–63
   leadership style of, 183–204
   managing of other managers by, 60–79
   middle, *see* Middle manager
   motivation in, 74–76
   promotability of, 142–162
   social responsibility of, 106
   technical competence of, 146
   see also Middle manager
Managerial grid
   action initiation and, 30
   leadership and, 30

INDEX

Managerial Grid, The, 30 n., 64
Managerial style
  in first-line supervisor, 2
  turnover and, 91
  see also Leadership style
Materials problems, informing superior about, 207–208
Maturity, in middle manager, 139
MBO, *see* Management by Objectives
McGregor, Douglas, 7n., 102
Mental attitude, pressures and, 19
Mergers and acquisitions, middle manager in, 45
Middle manager
  ability to judge people, 112
  adaptability of, 40–42
  "adolescence" of, 229
  alertness in, 95
  asset maximizing by, 227–229
  challenge to principles of, 86
  changed policies and, 80–82
  channels open to, 237–240
  communication abilities of, 57
  compromise by, 87–90
  conceptualization in, 112
  conceptual skills and, 46–48
  coordination factor and, 56–59
  daily activity vs. status of, 148
  decentralization and, 44–45
  delegation by, 49–52
  development plan for, 120–141
  disapproval of executive action by, 85
  double standard of, 103
  evaluation by group in company politics, 116
  fairness of, 79
  "force-fed growth" of, 233–236
  front-office contacts of, 155–159
  "getting material" problem of, 156–157
  growth needs of, 132–135
  information given to superior by, 206–209
  information sources for, 238
  innovation in, 39
  interdepartmental relationships and, 48–49
  interpersonal relationships and, 69

255

Middle manager (*cont.*)
   isolation of, 82
   jealousy and, 67–68, 117–119
   job of, 39–59
   leadership style in, 183–204
   leadership tests for, 201–202
   learning process in, 49
   liabilities of, 230–233
   "losing cause" of, 84–85
   loyalty in, 108
   and Management by Objectives, 70–73
   managing of other managers by, 50–51
   maturity required in, 138–139
   in mergers and acquisitions, 45–46
   motivation in, 74–77
   negotiation and compromise by, 87–90
   new disciplines of, 53–54
   objectivity about subordinates in, 77–79
   occupational disease of, 80–99
   as "opportunist," 104–105
   opportunity recognition by, 240–241
   organizational structure and, 47
   peer relationships and, 41, 82, 163–182
   perception of subordinate's reactions by, 94
   performance review by superior, 219–222
   policy implementation by, 42–46
   popularity of, 149
   pressure coefficient of, 96–99
   reaction time of, 93–96
   record keeping by, 48
   responsibilities of, 43
   responsibility split-up by, 68
   ruthlessness in, 117–118
   self-analysis in, 132–133
   self-commitment to politics in, 107–110
   self-control in, 98, 177, 231–232
   socialization by, 180–181
   staff groups and, 41
   status of with group, 148–150
   status quo and, 43, 48, 80–81, 92–93
   study of group by, 90–93

Middle manager *(cont.)*
    subordinate conflict resolution by, 63–67
        cooperation in, 170–173
    subordinates' work coordinated by, 54–56
    support from superior, 222–225
    "surprising the boss" technique of, 84
    technical expertise of, 133
    threat to position and power of, 43–45, 80
    value judgments of, 15
    vested interests of, 90
    work-area changes and, 40–41
    work coordination by, 54–56
    see also Manager
Money, as motivation, 74
Money matters, informing superior of, 206–207
Motivation, types of, 74–77
Mouton, Jane S., 30 n., 64

National Labor Relations Board, 208
Negotiation, overestimating in, 87
Nervous tics, 19
New disciplines, management of, 52–54
New employees, leadership style and, 198

Objectives, management by, *see* Management by Objectives
Objectivity, about subordinates, 77–79
Off-the-job relationships, 180–181
On-the-job experience, in development plan, 135
Opportunism, 104–105
Opportunity
    creativity and, 241–242
    recognition of by first-line supervisor, 240–241
Organization, loyalty to, 108
Organizational planning, ambition and, 36
Organizational structure
    conceptual skills and, 46–47
    middle manager's position in, 47
Organizational studies, 91
Overtime
    by first-line supervisor, 22–25
    health and, 24

Peer group
    attitude toward, 25–28
    competition from, 26
    good will of, 149
    as individuals, 27
Peer relationships, 163–182
    character assassination in, 118–119
    communication and, 216–217
    cooperation in, 170–173
    development plan and, 130
    discipline and control in, 179
    double standard in, 103
    enemies in, 173–176
    friendship and, 164
    hostility in, 174
    leadership style and, 194–197
    Machiavellianism and, 102–103
    off-the-job, 180–182
    reputation and, 166
    promotability and, 146–149
    self-control in, 177, 179
    socialization and, 180–181
    study of other managers in, 179
    supervisory performance and, 172
    trust and, 166–170
    working climate and, 28
Performance review, by superior, 219–222
Personalities, in negotiation and compromise, 89
Personnel problems, informing superior about, 208
Plan, development, *see* Development plan
Policy implementation, by middle manager, 42–46
Politics, 100–120
    ability to judge people in, 112
    alliance with "candidate" in, 113
    allies in, 114–117
    decision making and innovation in, 111–112
    executive potential and, 112–114
    intelligence sources in, 109
    jealousy in, 117–119
    killer instinct in, 117–120
    and loyalty, 108
    "picking winner" in, 111–114

INDEX

Politics, 100–120 (*cont.*)
  and promotion, 111
  ruthlessness in, 117
  self-commitment in, 107–110
  superior as antagonist in, 110
  upward mobility and, 111
  wife's involvement in, 158
Popularity, promotability and, 149
Power drive, as motivation, 75
Preparedness, ambition and, 35
Pressure
  business ethics and, 103–107
  functioning under, 20–21
  health and, 19, 24, 97
  interpersonal relationships and, 98
  mental attitude and, 19
Pressure coefficient, 42, 96–99
Prestige, as motivation, 76
Price fixing, ethics of, 106
Prince, The (Machiavelli), 100
Production cost, control of, 5–7, 220
Production standards, 5
Promotability
  administrative record in, 152–154
  "clean" rating in, 152–155
  and competition, 144–145
  evidence of, 142–162
  flexibility and, 147
  front-office contacts and, 155–159
  "getting noticed" problem in, 156–157
  good will and, 149
  inventiveness and, 241
  knowledge of competition and, 144–145
  leadership and, 147
  management by objectives and, 143
  past grievances as factor in, 148, 152–153
  peer status and, 146–149
  performance review in, 159
  personal relationships and, 147
  readiness and, 159–161
  record-keeping and, 153–154
  self-rating in, 148

Promotability *(cont.)*
   status and, 148–150
   technical competence and, 146
Promotion
   added responsibility in, 20
   available candidates for, 145
   company politics and, 111
   dangers in, 160
   factors in, 143–144
   future prospects and, 243–245
   hints and allusions of, 212–214
   knowledge required for, 159–160
   leadership style and, 186
   as motivation, 75
   planning for, 16–17
   promises of from superior, 212–214
   readiness for, 159–161
   superior's support in, 222–225
Public relations, first-line supervisor and, 7

Reaction time, of middle manager, 93–96
Record keeping, promotability and, 153–154
Reeves, E. T., 176 n.
Reputation, peer relationships and, 166
Responsibility
   competition and, 26
   increase or decrease in, 18–38
   promotion and, 20
   and tension, 18–19
Ruthlessness, in middle management, 117

Secrecy, in supervisory relationships, 209–210
Self-confidence, strengthening of, 132
Self-control
   feedback in, 232
   importance of in development program, 231
   and leadership style, 193
   in middle manager, 98
   in peer relationships, 177
Self-development
   leadership style and, 200–204
   plans for, *see* Development plan

Self-image, leadership style and, 190–191
Self-rating, promotability and, 148
Seminars
　in development plan, 136–137
　proprietary, 139
Sensitivity training, in development plan, 132–133
Socialization, peer relationships and, 180–181
Social responsibility, of management, 106
Status
　backlash and, 151
　promotability and, 148–150
Status quo
　vs. change, 43, 80–82
　maintenance of, 81, 92
　reaction to change in, 93
　threat to, 43, 80
Stress, adrenaline production in, 19
Subordinate(s)
　vs. "associate" or "colleague," 101–102
　conflict among, 63–65
　delegation to, 51
　fairness to, 79
　jealousy in, 67–68
　leadership style and, 197–200
　manager's impact on, 190–192
　objectivity about, 77–79
　perception of reactions in, 94
　rating of manager by, 148–151
　of rival in company politics, 119
　trust of, 187–190
　work coordination among, 55
Superior
　avoidance of, 32–34
　compromise with, 89
　control by, 32–34
　in development plan, 136
　as father figure, 33
　hints of promotion for, 212–214
　information given to manager from, 209–212
　information received by, 206–209
　as kingpin in communications system, 215–216

261

Superior *(cont.)*
 knowledge of by subordinate, 218
 opposition to in management politics, 110
 performance review by, 219–222
 support from, 222–225
 "surprising" of, 84
 upward communication to, 215–217
Supervisor
 communication from, 205–225
 first-line, *see* First-line supervisor
Supervisory predictability, 184

Technology, channels of advancement in, 239
Tension, responsibility and, 18–19
Theory X and Theory Y, 7, 102
Tickler files, information from, 57, 155
Toastmasters' clubs, 132, 139
Trust
 betrayal of, 237
 communication and, 189–190
 feedback in, 168
 peer relationships and, 166–170
 of subordinates, 187–190
Tunnel vision, 9, 90, 92, 240
Turnover, managerial style and, 91

Ulcers, pressure and, 97
Unfriendliness, among peers, 25
Upward mobility, politics and, 111

Value judgments
 in development plan, 141
 in middle manager's job, 15

Wife, in company politics, 158
Work, continuity in, 40
Work area, middle manager and, 40–41
Work coordination, by middle manager, 54–56
Work experience, promotion and, 144
Work force, first-line supervisor and, 2
 see also Subordinate